KU-627-541

THROUGH FRANCE TO THE MED.

THROUGH FRANCE TO THE MED.

Any Yachtsman's Attainable Dream

MIKE HARPER

Gentry Books : London

First Published 1974
© Mike Harper 1974
ISBN 0 85614 034 1

All rights reserved. Without written permission from Gentry Books Limited, this volume, or any part of it, may not be reproduced by any means or in any form.

Published by Gentry Books Limited
15, Tooks Court, London, EC4A 1LA
Printed by Lowe & Brydone (Printers) Ltd.,
London · Thetford

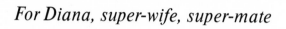

For Diana, super-wife, super-mate

Acknowledgements

I would like to thank the editors of Yachting and Boating Weekly and Motor Boat and Yachting for kind permission to reproduce material which has already appeared in their publications, and the French Government Tourist Office and the Spanish Government Tourist Office as well as the Gibraltar Tourist Office for their help in supplying many of the photographs which appear in this book.

The author and publishers have taken every care to ensure that the facts in this book are accurate and up to date, but in view of the constantly changing situation in the many places described in the book and the lapse of time between preparing copy for the printers and actual publication, can accept no responsibility for any error which may have crept in.

Contents

Illustrations

Let the Walter Mitty inside you fight his way out.
Inside most of us there is a Walter Mitty figure struggling to get out.

Don't you often day-dream?

If you are a yachting person don't you find yourself day-dreaming wildly improbable adventures?

There you are, a hundred feet above the deck of a square-rigger doubling the Horn, furling the main topgallant, and it doesn't affect the dream at all that you are not quite certain which sail *is* in fact the main topgallant, the name is enough. The wind is howling, a real Southerly Buster, and the great greybeards of seas are rolling up inexorably astern. On the deck the Captain debates with the Mate.

'Better promote young Smith to Second Mate, Mister,' he growls. 'We need a reliable man on deck in these waters and I can't see Whistleblower lasting long.'

Or do you dream of following in the wake of Slocum and the Hiscocks, of Moitessier and Rose, of Chichester and Knox-Johnston, sailing through enchanted blue waters, where the Trade Winds blow and the sea birds cry and the next land-fall is a thousand miles away?

It would be a poor world if one couldn't indulge oneself in these flights of fancy, and an even poorer one if there was no prospect at all of achieving even a modest yachting adventure, something a little more ambitious than the annual cruise.

That is what this book is all about. There is one yachting adventure which *is* attainable. It is a dream which many people have, simply because it is modest, it is an adventure because it is so much more than the annual cruise. It doesn't imply that one has the resources – physical, mental, financial – of the great adventurers of the yachting scene, though most of them have been humble men with little in the way of money.

What they have all had in common is a tremendous sense of purpose, a restless driving urge which compels them to go right ahead and do what they want to do.

In this book I am thus writing about a relatively minor exploit, one within the reach of pretty well everyone who has a little determination, some experience of messing about in boats, and of course, a boat. Its achievement is within the reach of most of us: the satisfaction to be experienced from doing it is tremendous.

The attainable dream – what is it?

It is the trip through the canals and into the Med. and back home again. A trip which a surprisingly large number of people actually make. Through the French canals, an adventure in its own right, a cruise through the blue waters of the Mediterranean and the return passage home via the Canal du Midi, through the top half of the Bay of Biscay and home by way of the Channel Islands. Sailing in the Med. is a joy you have to experience to appreciate, and the return trip through the Canal du Midi induces a mental tranquility which softens the blow of having to come home and sets you up for the passage through the Bay, whose reputation is worse than its reality.

The Channel Islands, which lie naturally on the route, are worth visiting anyway, especially in the autumn, the time of year when you will be on your way home.

This is what this book is all about. We are agreed on the nature of the attainable dream: this book attempts to tell you what is involved in making it come true.

There is only one problem with which it cannot help you. That is making the decision for you to chuck in your job and set off. The determination to do just that, to hurdle this barrier, this calls for a determination as great as that which has possessed the great yachting adventurers. And when you have read this book it may be that making the great decision will be easier than you thought.

1. Planning Preparation

"Plan your work: work your plan" — well-worn cliche

"Be yare in thy preparation, for thy assailant is quick, skilful and deadly" — William Shakespeare.

PLANNING

I sometimes brood upon the number of people who set off on ambitious voyages and give up for some reason within twenty miles of the starting point. One yacht I heard of set off from the Thames to go round the world and hit a buoy at Gravesend and got no further!

How many dream trips never even get as far as that? A large number I suspect, and the probable reason is that they were not properly planned. It's no good just going, you have to work it all out beforehand.

Most worthwhile human activities happen because they are planned, and the more complex the project the greater the necessity to plan.

The sequence of events is to set an objective and then work out a programme which will enable you to achieve it. Then work your programme and modify it in the light of what actually happens, and usually it is best to break the main objective down into a series of limited objectives which become the steps in the programme.

This is what management by objectives is all about, and the basic principles apply to organising the attainment of the dream. If you have the right sort of mind you can even set up the programme in the form of critical path analysis!

15

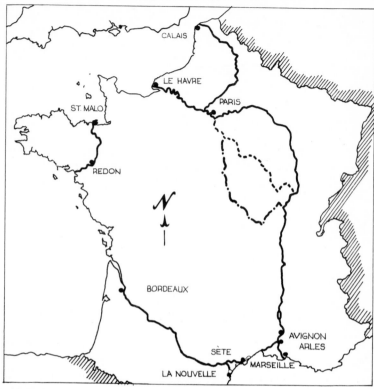

Solid lines show recommended routes across France. Most of the canals have been omitted for clarity. You can enter the system at Calais or at Le Havre, and from Paris have the choice of three routes. The one suggested is not the shortest but it is probably the easiest and most pleasant. The solid line running in a north-westerly direction from the Mediterranean is the Canal du Midi and the Canal Latèral a la Garonne, and the short cut which is only open to smaller yachts which by-passes the trip around Ushant is also shown by a solid line.

One way of applying this to the dream is to make an enormous list and work through it. What goes on the list? This is what we are going to discuss now.

Have you a boat? Is it suitable for this kind of voyage? A lot of nonsense is written about boats which are suitable for cruising. What you need is a boat which is large enough for you and your crew to be able to live in comfortably for several months, seaworthy enough to cope with the kind of sea and weather conditions we experience in home waters. The

engine must be reliable and must be accessible for maintenance, spares must be available from the manufacturer, and
you must be able to carry enough fuel to cover 200 miles at
normal cruising speed. She must be sound and adequately
equipped. And to achieve the dream the dimensions must not
exceed 98ft. 5ins. in length, 16ft. 5ins. in the beam, and 5ft.
3ins. draught, otherwise she will be unable to negotiate the
canals. Equally important is a dimension which you will
probably have to check, and that is the height above the
waterline – 11ft. 2ins. at the centre and 7ft. 6ins. at the
sides. The figures which apply to the Breton canals and rivers
are – 85ft. 3ins. length, 14ft. 9ins. beam, 4ft. 1in. draught and
8ft. 2ins. at centre, 7ft. 6ins. at the sides above the water.

These are the official dimensions and it is best to accept
them as accurate because even half an inch could involve you
in a catastrophe.

The next major issue is that of money. What is it going to
cost? Obviously this is going to vary very much from
individual to individual, because our boats and their running
costs are so different and our own personal tastes vary so
much. Most people I know can manage without caviare or gin
and tonic: but not every one!

But many of the costs can be estimated with some
accuracy. As a working budget figure it is quite possible to
manage a six-month trip through the canals and back with
three months in the Med. for under £1000. This is excluding
loss of earnings while you are away, and assumes frugal
tastes.

Before discusssing the budget in depth it is as well to
consider the itinerary in greater detail. Without doing this it
is impossible to estimate your fuel bill, list the charts, pilot
books and so on which you will need and these are all factors
which affect the budget.

In addition you will be unable to list the documents you
will require, you won't be able to advise your friends where
to contact you or arrange for any to join you as paying
(handsomely I hope) guests. You won't be able to arrange to
pick up your job again on your return unless you can give the
boss a fairly realistic date, and you won't be able to go at all
unless you set a firm departure date to which you intend to

keep, and then work backwards to fix deadlines for the various tasks to be completed as part of your preparations.

So set a departure date for as early in the spring as you dare, a return date as late as you dare, and then fill in between as realistically as you can.

General layout of the Western Mediterranean — pause here and let your imagination wander a little!

The trip splits itself up logically into:-

UK to France
Through the canals
Med. – outward part of the trip
Med. – homeward part of the trip
Through the canals to Bordeaux
Back to the UK

...art of the valley of the Seine: Petit Andely, where weeping willows and churches ...ne the banks of the river.
...icture: Jonathan Eastland)

It is a good idea to allow adequate time to pass through the canals. There is a considerable physical and mental strain involved in the route to the Med. and it can be quite exhausting if you attempt to break records, especially if you are crewing with just your wife or girl-friend.

But if you take your time you can get a lot of enjoyment out of seeing a part of France which is nearly all so much off the beaten track that very few visitors ever see it. The route runs through a variety of countrysides, ranging from the

Le Quai des Elysee in Paris: just some of the yachts tied up at the Port de Plaisance. There will be room here for you too.
(picture: Jonathan Eastland)

beautiful valley of the Seine to the rural loneliness of the canals in the centre of the country. It takes you through the heart of Paris, though it is hard to imagine any route through France which failed to do just that! It takes you through Lyons, Avignon, Arles, Rouen, Chalons-sur-Saône, to list just a few of the larger towns, and a host of fascinating small villages, including places so rustic that chickens still run in the streets and into the houses. The return route too runs through an area of tremendous interest.

So, please, don't waste the opportunity which the inland waters part of the trip gives to you.

This is the actual timetable I kept to when my wife and I lived the dream a year or so ago:-

April	25	left Thames
May	8	left Honfleur on the mouth of the Seine
	12	arrived Paris
	15	left Paris
June	3	arrived Lyons
	5	left Lyons
	7	arrived Med.
	12	arrived Port Cros
	16	left Port Cros
	19	arrived Agde
	30	arrived Barcelona
July	11	arrived Alicante
	17	arrived Almeria
	20	arrived Gibraltar
	25	arrived Tangier
	27	arrived Mdiq
	28	arrived Gibraltar
August	8	arrived Alicante
	11	arrived Cala Yondal, Ibiza
	22	arrived Port Andraitx, Mallorca
	25	arrived Palma, Mallorca
September	6	left Soller, Mallorca
	12	arrived Agde
	21	arrived Toulouse
	28	arrived Bordeaux
October	6	arrived Audierne

	14	arrived St Peter Port, Guernsey
	20	arrived Cherbourg
	22	arrived Yarmouth, Isle of Wight
	31	arrived Dover
November	5	arrived on Thames

There are one or two lessons to be learnt from this time-table. We started out late, mainly due to engine troubles which could not have been anticipated and which I was glad happened when they did! We attempted to cover too much ground in the Med. We stayed in one or two places longer than was really justified, for personal reasons like sickness or renewing friendships. Reserve time has to be built into your itinerary to allow for these.

If we had fallen badly behind schedule we could have cut out the whole of the diversion to Gib., Tangier and even the whole of the trip to the Balearics.

The north face of the Rock of Gibraltar floodlit. You will want to stay here fo.
a day or two if you possibly can.
(picture: Gibraltar Tourist Office)

22

ACTION POINT. If you are really serious about undertaking a trip like this – sit down right now with a piece of paper and a map and work out your own programme.

Make sure that it is realistic when related to the cruising speed of your boat. Make sure that your plan doesn't mean that you spend all your time travelling.

Don't anticipate making any really long hops between harbours, unless this is the kind of yachting which you enjoy. The way we did the trip we had every night in bed in port or in an anchorage, except for the night passage back from Mallorca to the Spanish mainland. The result of making hops which are too long is that you are often too tired when you make port to enjoy your stay there – and when you are rested it will be time to move on again if the programme is too tight.

The reason we turned left on entering the Med. before retracing our footsteps and running down the Spanish coast was to give ourselves an opportunity to visit the fascinating islands near Marseilles known as the Iles d'Hyères. If you continue east from there you may find yourself having to put into expensive harbours which are so fashionable that you may be unable to find a berth! By heading west from Iles d'Hyères you run down the Spanish coast, where there are plenty of harbours, and where nothing is so expensive.

By heading west you give yourself the opportunity also to go to such fascinating places as Gibraltar, Tangier and the Balearics.

Having worked out your programme, check on how long you have allowed yourself for each stage of the trip. If like me, you want to spend every night in harbour, by following my route there should be no need to do anything different. There are always harbours within an easy day's sail or motor from each other.

You will find in the Med. that the extreme heat, more acute the further south you get, will tend to sap your energy and that you will be reluctant to make long passages, so don't be too ambitious in your programming.

You should also remember that the winds of the Med. are notoriously fickle, and if you are sailing you are very unlikely to cover as much ground as in home waters. There is usually no wind, too much wind, or some wind in the wrong direction, and this is not just a cynicism.

Remember too that an excessively lengthy itinerary is going to add to the cost of the trip because you are going to use more fuel.

Now that you have prepared your draft itinerary let us think more deeply about what it is all going to cost.

This is the actual budget for my trip in 1969:-

Fuel and lubricating oil	£73
Food taken with us	143
Charts, Pilots, Books	49
Insurance on boat	58
Insurance – personal accident	32
New warps, chandlery	16
Engine spares	54
Batteries, bulbs, grease, etc.	10
Coal, miscellaneous	10
New sail	11
Seafix D/F	28
Spending money (includes Rhône pilot, harbour dues, fresh food)	220
Films and developing	40
Scaffold boards, pickets	7
Rockets, safety equipment	18
	£769
plus inflation allowance for 1974	231
	£1000

Before discussing these figures in detail it would be a good idea to think about what is usually described as putting one's affairs in order. By this I mean making a will, giving someone – probably the executor of your will – a power of attorney over your affairs, including the right to draw cheques on your bank account and even overdraw it, and ensuring that any standing orders paid by your bank, like life policy premiums, are covered by income while you are away.

This is not being melodramatic. It is being wise, because accidents can and do occur, and you must try to be in the best possible situation if something does go wrong.

Now let's see how the figures quoted above came to be so large!

Fuel and lubricating oil. This is a figure which can be estimated with some degree of accuracy, providing you know just how many gallons per hour your engine consumes on

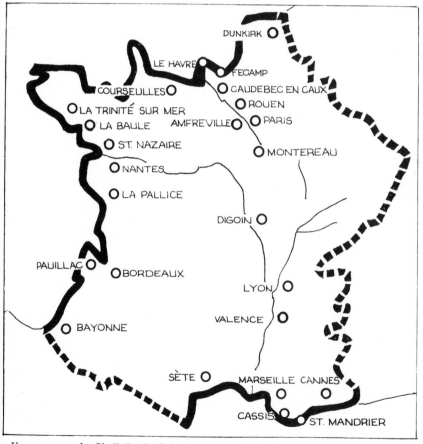

You can use the Shell Credit Scheme at any of the places shown on this map.

average. How many miles do you think you will cover under power? Apart from the canal sections, which must be taken slowly and therefore at an economical speed, allow a generous margin, because the chances are that the lack of favourable sailing winds in the Med. − if yours is a sailing boat − will result in your spending far more time under power than you anticipate.

My own experience is that the wind is normally on the nose if it is there at all, and that it stays on the nose when you round a headland and expect to find it on the beam!

Payment for fuel bought abroad is best done under the Shell Credit Scheme. This enables you to take on diesel fuel against a Letter of Credit. Payment is made by Shell debiting your bank account at home so that no cash changes hands, which has the benefit of reducing your reliance upon hard cash and travellers cheques. The scheme only operates at specified ports, but there are plenty of them, and it is easy to organise your re-fuelling so that you always do it at one of them.

Anything which you can do to reduce the amount of money you need to have around at any time is worth bothering about, especially if you are going to places where the honesty of the inhabitants is less than guaranteed.

If you have an income which continues while you are away, like a pension or dividends on shares, you may be able to organise matters so that your fuelling costs are covered by income.

Food taken with us. How can two people think that they are going to eat so much tinned stuff in six months? The appendix lists what we actually took, and the list was based on the assumption that it would be cheaper to buy food in bulk and store it on the boat rather than buy it from day to day abroad.

What you can take depends a great deal on the volume of stowage space in the boat and on the kind of food you enjoy. We have a dietary peculiarity which probably won't apply to you: we don't eat meat. This resulted in our not having to take cases of corned beef and spam or whatever and it also meant that our bill was less than it would have been if we had taken tinned meats because meat is a very expensive item, certainly more expensive than the kind of things we do eat, like cheese, fish, soya bean products and so on.

The best way to buy the food you take with you is to go to a cash and carry wholesale warehouse and buy in cased lots at wholesale prices. You should save at least ten per cent this way: more on many items.

Many of these establishments operate a strictly 'Trade only' policy, some are less scrupulous, and you may have to shop around a little. The answer to probing questions is that you are a caterer.

The problem in shopping in a cash and carry warehouse is that it is easy to be carried away by the strange environment and load up the trolley with vast quantities of food, forgetting that some cases contain 24 tins, even 36 or 48! My classic mistake was buying a catering pack of custard powder, seven pounds in weight, enough to make several hundred gallons, according to my wife.

The catering packs are often worth selecting, however. Squash by the gallon, cooking oil by the gallon, detergent by the gallon and disinfectant by the gallon, these are usually good buys. Dehydrated vegetables in catering packs, packet soups in catering sizes, jams and marmalades in large tins, all are worth thinking about.

So this is where you need to draw up the biggest shopping list of your life.

Admiralty Pilots very helpful, because they are not written *Charts, Pilots, Books.* We spent more on charts than we needed to have done, because we originally intended to return from the Med. by going round the Iberian peninsula, and thus we have a load of charts which have never been used. The price of charts has gone up since we bought them, though.

There are certain essential books, such as *Reeds Almanac,* which you must have, though one reason for writing this book is to reduce the number. We have never found Admiralty Pilots very helpful, because they are not written for people with small boats and their advice is not very relevant. They are also very much out of date, especially the drawings of conspicuous features, most of which now seem to have been hidden by new hotels!

Two books we didn't take and regretted having forgotten were a good book on medical matters and a good book on the flora and fauna of the places we visited. There are so many trees, plants, birds, fish and insects which are indigenous to the places on the route and which were new to us that we were very sorry to be unable to identify them or learn anything about them.

Insurance. Some people never insure their boats for normal cruising: I think they must be nuts. Some people will no doubt follow the same policy when they make their dream trip and they will be even nuttier. In order to make the journey through the French inland water-ways you *must* be insured and even if this were not the case it would be daft to make this trip uninsured.

A frail yacht can easily find herself in one of the larger locks between two barges, one on each side, and if it is a lock with sloping sides and you are descending the inevitable result is that the barges converge on each other, with you in the middle. Although it is highly unlikely that a lock-keeper would put a yacht in this situation unless he knew that there was enough clearance to compensate for the distance the barges moved inwards, well, accidents have been known to happen.

The Med. itself is far from being the tranquil mill-pond it is often alleged to be so the usual yachting hazards can be anticipated. The return trip round the coast of Brittany takes one through some of the most treacherous waters in the world, and although normal prudent seamanship will overcome the problems it is stupid not to be insured.

What the premium will be depends on your boat and its value and the kind of deal your broker can negotiate. The older the boat the greater the problem of getting her insured. A forty-year-old lifeboat conversion may be difficult for the broker to arrange! If you are still deciding what sort of boat to buy this is a point to bear in mind.

Whether or not to take out personal accident insurance is a personal decision. I would advocate doing so because the consequences of an accident can be far worse and very expensive when you are out of the UK compared with the same thing at home even though the chances of having one are no greater. Far from home, no friends, no one to love you, no free National Health Scheme, no reserve of money, no job. . . . . .

When we were in Palma, Mallorca, we had occasion to utilize the services of a doctor. The yacht club was very helpful in giving us the name of a doctor who spoke English, and although his fees were reasonable and the cost of having his prescription made up was also reasonable we had to settle on the spot. Reimbursement was delayed until after our return to the UK some three months later.

This didn't help at all as far as the problem of finding the money at the time was concerned, even though the arrival of the cheque not long after our return − when we had no jobs and no income − came at a highly propitious time.

A word of caution about personal accident insurance. Read the fine print! They won't pay out for a claim for what they describe as a pre-existent disease or complaint.

Rope, chandlery. What you spend on these items depends on you. Make sure that your boat is well-equipped. To replace gear which is broken or stolen may not be easy while you are away and it will almost certainly be expensive. We will discuss this in some detail later on.

Engine spares. Some manufacturers hire out a set of spares and special tools for a long trip and at the end you return what is left. This is a good idea. Others have such a good distribution system for spares that you should always be able to get out of trouble no matter what and no matter where.

If you are a good engineer you may do better by taking a carefully selected set of spares with you and doing it all your self.

In any case regular and careful maintenance of the engine throughout the trip is essential. Whether or not you do this yourself of rely on local agents and marine engineers is a matter for you to decide, but local labour is likely to be expensive − and they may not have had previous experience with your particular engine.

You are quite likely to have to call upon local resources at some stage for help, so that an essential item to add to your list is the engine manufacturer's book of agents and distributors as well as the manual for the engine and the spares list. Many manufacturers are very helpful with free advice, and some run short courses in their factories to train mechanics – if you are going to be completely reliant on power it might be a very good idea to attend one of these courses.

When approaching the manufacturer for the spares list and so on it is also a good idea to give him a copy of your proposed itinerary and ask whether the changing ambient conditions will mean making any adjustments to fuel, lubricants and cooling system. In the heat of the Med. the engine compartment may well require additional ventilation.

And you may decide that your spanner sets are not quite adequate – so check up that you have enough of the right sizes in ring, open-ended and socket varieties. An enormous Stillson wrench is a good standby for emergency and a good heavy-duty vice is also important.

Grease, bulbs, batteries. You need all kinds of grease – grease for the engine, grease for the water pump, grease for glands; you need spare batteries for radios and echo-sounders and torches; you need spare bulbs for torches, searchlights, navigation lights and cabin lights. It is better to take these things with you because you may have difficulty finding the correct replacements abroad.

We overdid things when stocking up on these items. Bulbs don't burn out all that often and it is surprising just how long batteries do last. And we never did use the fuse wire.

Coal, miscellaneous. You are going to need some form of heating on board. The *mistral* is a cold wind, and on the homeward trip you are going to run into chilly autumnal nights. So you need some form of instant heat. We have a small caravan-type solid fuel fire, hence the item for coal.

A good alternative for small yachts is a Camping Gaz fire and a supply of cartridges. Spare cylinders are obtainable in most places, but if you can afford the space it is better to take the spares with you, not only in case they are out of stock when you go shopping, but also because currency fluctuations may make it cheaper to take them.

If you cook by paraffin you would do better with a fire which uses the same fuel.

Included under 'miscellaneous' is a 100ft length of hose and the kind of tap fitting which caters for various sizes of tap, plus two plastic five-gallon jerricans, for humping water when the hose won't reach.

Water is not always easily obtainable and you must have alternative means of getting it on board.

New sail. This is an item which many people can cross off the list straight away, but its presence serves as a reminder to you to remember to check out all the gear, and replace any sails and so on which you have been promising to get for some time but have been deferring – now you can justify spending the money!

Under 'sail' you can include 'awning'. The sun in the Med. is so hot that everybody sets up awnings to shield themselves – and the boat – from its direct rays. Without an awning the accommodation gets so hot that sleep is almost impossible.

It also provides shade for your afternoon siesta on deck – a Mediterranean custom well worth adopting – and there will be times when you will be glad to sleep under it at night, using it to shield you from the dew.

An awning doesn't have to be very expensive. A square of canvas or a rectangle is all that is needed, with eyelets along the edges to enable you to lash it, and these are sold cheaply by the tarpaulin manufacturers who advertise in the *Exchange & Mart.* Specially shaped awnings are expensive.

A wind scoop to fit the portholes, especially in the sleeping cabin, is also virtually essential. You can make one yourself with a little ingenuity. All it has to do is deflect whatever breeze there may be into the cabin.

While on the subject of special gear for the Med. let us think about the special gangplank you will have to take with you to enable you to get ashore when moored in the normal Mediterranean fashion, stern-to. This can take the form of a scaffold plank which stands on a rubber mat on your tran-

This is how they usually tie up in the Med. — stern to, with gang-planks which rise and fall with the movement of the yachts.
(picture: Malta Government Tourist Board)

som, lashed to your boat, which spans the gap from boat to quay, or it can be a specially made device with gimbals which retracts by pulling it up on the backstay or a special halliard. The expensive gin palaces in the slick Mediterranean marinas have some very sophisticated devices indeed.

The advantage of the gangplank made out of a scaffold board is that it is simple, strong, and can double as an orthodox gangplank when tied up in the canals, acting at the same time as a sprague to keep the boat off the bank.

By slipping rubber tyres over the ends it will serve as a very heavy-duty fender in harbours where dolphins project from the wall and normal fenders are virtually useless, especially in any kind of a swell.

The plank should have wooden treads nailed across it every foot or so to provide grip when wet or at an angle.

There is an alternative which overcomes the problems of weight inherent with the scaffold board, which is very unwieldy and almost unmanageable when you have only one end to grip! The alternative is a light aluminium ladder with canvas stretched along its length. The canvas must be stitched on very well and stretched very tight so that it will support one's weight.

The cost of scaffold boards is included under the heading 'scaffold boards and pickets', so don't include them twice on your check list.

Seafix D/F. It is very easy to get carried away by thoughts of the impending passage and start spending large sums of money on navigational equipment. In addition to a good and reliable compass, which you have had swung, the most important item is a radio direction finder. The Seafix is the one I use and would recommend. It is not expensive, is accurate enough for yachtsmen, and has the virtue of being able to be used as a visual hand-bearing compass as well as for taking D/F bearings.

If you don't have a D/F already the cost of the Seafix is well justified.

In my view there is little need for an echo sounder, little for radar, none for an automatic pilot, and most of the other exotic electronic devices on the market which are of most use to people who go offshore racing or deep sea cruising.

I am assuming that you will be able to take a reasonable transistor radio with you to receive weather forecasts. If you intend to buy one it is worth thinking about getting one which will receive signals from D/F beacons – there is a cheap Russian one at around £14 which will do just that. You could use this in an emergency as a substitute for the Seafix, with not so much accuracy, but enough to get yourself out of trouble.

If you don't have them already you will need a pair of dividers, parallel rules, rubbers, pencils, Douglas protractors and so on.

Spending money. How on earth did we manage to spend £220? Well, it includes £26 for the Rhône pilot – more about

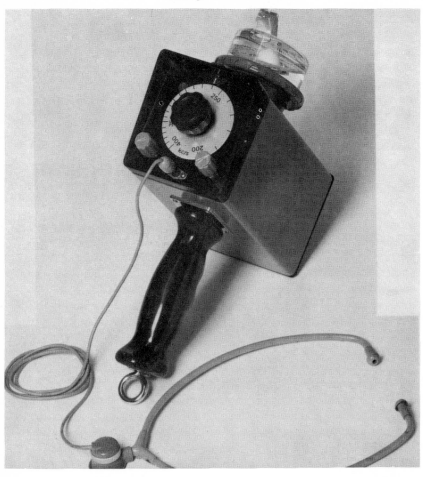

A Seafix D/F set. You can see the hand-bearing compass on top easily.

him later — and £11 for harbour dues. Most of this was paid in England and it includes port dues as well as mooring charges.

The yachtsman is not charged for the use of the French canal system, which is generous in the extreme. Often no charge is made in European harbours for the first night's stay, but payment is made thereafter, which is another inducement to keep moving!

English harbour dues are very expensive compared with

similar harbours in France and Spain, though there are signs, alas, that the others are beginning to catch up.

If you stay odd nights in marinas you will find that you are spending more money than you have budgeted for, so cross the Channel as quickly as you can and try not to spend nights in harbours where the only berthing available to yachts is in marinas.

Very often it is possible to anchor safely close to the shore, and it is seldom that this costs anything.

Also included in the £220 is the cost of buying fresh food during our travels. Eggs, fruit, vegetables, all have to be bought. Meat, too, if you eat it, an item which is rapidly approaching the luxury food class. Fish is included in the £220 and this is often very cheap in fishing harbours.

Probably £100 is the cost of fresh food included in the £220. For two people for six months this is really not bad! You can often save money by buying food which is plentiful and cheap in the particular locality in which you find yourself and stockpiling it if possible. Melons are cheap in Spain and North Africa, wine is cheap on the continent generally, sardines are cheap in Gibraltar. Don't forget that shopping in markets abroad is often just as sensible as it is in the UK.

Surprisingly, the £220 includes very little spent on entertainment, eating out, presents, and includes nothing on cigarettes. It does include out of pocket daily expenses like bottles of wine, and postcards, which it is difficult not to send, but which add to one's living cost incredibly rapidly.

Films and developing. You are sure to want to make a permanent record of the trip. Because of its nature it is most likely that you will want it to be in colour, whether in the form of prints, transparencies, or movies. None of these is cheap, but it may be possible to save a little by buying in bulk and negotiating a discount.

Scaffold boards and pickets. We have already discussed scaffold boards, but what are pickets? Nothing to do with Union action, pickets are the heavy iron bars with an eye at one end and a sharpened point at the other, which are used on building sites to suspend the ropes which mark off restricted areas.

You just drive them into the ground with a sledge hammer when you want to tie up for the night on a stretch of canal bank where there are no trees or other solid things to which you can attach your lines. The mooring screws offered for light cruisers on UK rivers and canals are useless on the Continent because the surge of the barge traffic will pull your boat along and up-root the rigging screws.

A sledge hammer is not really essential for driving in the pickets. Canal banks are usually pretty soft, and I found a 2lb hammer, which is part of the engine-room tool-kit, quite adequate.

Equally essential for canal work is a large pile of old motor tyres, which shouldn't cost you anything. The dumpy ones are best.

You cut a hole in them with a brace and bit to act as a drain hole, and two more holes opposite the drain hole to pass the line through, so that it won't chafe between the boat and the side of a lock.

And then you make sure that you have enough tyres on board virtually to cover the whole length of the boat, both sides, at water-line level and at rubbing-strake level, so that when you start the canal-bashing part of the trip you are well protected.

The boat is bound to take a hammering in the locks. Apart from the problems of being in the same large locks as the large commercial barges — the *peniches* — there are so many of the small locks to get through that even though you will have them to yourself you will be bound to rub against a knuckle or brush against a wall, and without good protection the paint will suffer badly — and that may be the least damage you have inflicted on the boat.

Some people advocate covering the sides of the boat with polythene sheeting and using the tyres to keep it in place, and this strikes me as a good idea.

Rockets, safety equipment. This is just plain prudence. Larger yachts, those of 45ft. or over, are required by law to carry certain life-saving equipment, and when undertaking a six-month trip it is wise for smaller yachts to do the same. We took a Schermuly Yachtpack, which contains a very good selection of flares in a watertight polythene container.

We also took five lifejackets, two for us and three for our friends. Each lifejacket has a whistle attached to it by a lanyard, plus a bulb powered by a battery which is only activated by immersion in salt water.

On many boats life lines and harness are essential.

A radar reflector and a medicine chest are essential too. An anchor 'shape' is a good thing to have on board.

This concludes the explanation of where all the money went. Experience suggests one or two more items are worth mentioning.

These include a boat-hook — two if you have room on board. One should be long, very stout, and have a good double hook on the end, while the other should be short and light and only need have one hook. Usually I am against boat-hooks, because they can turn into weapons whose offensive powers equal the lances of Mediaeval times which they so much resemble. It is normally possible to manoeuvre a yacht so that the use of a boat-hook is unnecessary, but for canal work there are times when you may find a boat-hook very useful indeed, especially for pushing the yacht off the mud along the banks if you try to tie up at a place where there is less water than you anticipated. The short one is for fishing things out of the water and picking up buoys in situations when the wind and lack of room to manoeuvre make it impossible to get close enough to the buoy to pick it up by hand.

Torches and searchlights are items I don't feel I have stressed sufficiently.

A good torch is an essential item on any yacht's inventory, one which can double as a signalling lamp, is powerful enough to act as a searchlight, and which floats. If you pass through the tunnel near Balesmes, which is nearly three miles long, you will need a good torch to enable you to see the sides and the barge in front.

Courtesy flags are also good things to take with you. I am not one of the subscribers to the 'flags at sunset' school, believing that many of the world's troubles are caused by nationalism and that flags are just one of its manifestations, but it is courteous to fly the flag of the country whose hospitality you are accepting and lack of the flag may upset patriotic officials in some ports who can retaliate quite easily and effectively by just being unco-operative.

A good hooter is essential for advising lock-keepers in the less used canals that you are coming and would they please prepare the lock. This is not as vital as some people would tell you, because if you start the day well by getting on the right side of the keeper of the first lock you will find that each lock-keeper in turn will phone the next in line right down the canal. The sort of hooters the barges use can be heard miles off and cost a fortune. I suggest you shop around, and try to find a horn with a trumpet to direct its blast in the direction you wish your signal to be most audible.

Needless to say, when you pass through the canals your mast will have to be lowered and stowed on deck. This may involve the construction of some kind of crutch or trestle to support it clear of the deck above the coach-roof. You can probably knock up something suitable yourself out of an appropriately hefty piece of timber.

If you have a heavy boat, by which I mean in excess of say 12 tons, it is worth thinking of taking steel hawsers to act as warps in the canals, where the surge of the passing barges can snap a normal rope warp quite easily. This may seem bizarre advice but there were times when I watched my own heavy polypropylene warps stretch as much as a foot when a barge went past. The reason is that they take all the water with them so that the entire weight of the yacht is thrown on the warps. To take heavier than normal warps is one answer, but you may find that you are using ropes which are too big and heavy to be easy to handle.

These late thoughts are all prompted by experience of canal bashing, a subject to which I will return later.

There is a final thought on financial matters, which slots in here. You must have some reserve of funds on board in case of emergency. Most people who attain the dream have been people with slender resources, and it is a sad fact that a proportion of those who attempt it give up because some unforeseeable disaster found them without enough money to sort it out.

In Gibraltar, for example, we met a number of young would-be round-the-world voyagers of all nationalities who were sleeping on the beach and attempting desparately to find work of some kind, on a yacht, as a steward, deck-hand, cook, anything. They had run out of money, been forced to sell their yacht in order to have money to buy food, before reluctantly they set off to hitch-hike home.

A friend of ours, a young South African called Kevin, had left the steel yacht he had spent two years building himself to the tender mercies of a 'ship-keeper' in Tangier, while he came to Gib. to try to find work to enable him to resume his round-the-world voyage. In the end he sold her for £400, which was criminal.

Another fifty quid would have kept Kevin out of trouble, and this is the kind of emergency fund I advocate you should hide somewhere on board, part in cash and part in travellers cheques. Really you need enough in travellers cheques to cover your air fare back from the most expensive airport you are likely to have to use in case of trouble at home.

And the last thought before leaving the subject of money — don't forget that while you are away you will not be earning and it may take a week or two on your return before any cash actually finds its way into your hand. So add 'loss of earnings on your return' to the note you already have.

ACTION POINT. Sit down and work out a budget. Check it out to make sure it is realistic.

ACTION POINT. Work out a check list for the food items you want to take with you and cost it out. Does it tally with the budget figure?

ACTION POINT. Make a master list of equipment you will have to buy. Compare it with the suggestions in this chapter.

ACTION POINT. Make a master list of things which have to be done before you go.

PREPARATION

Now we can delve a little deeper into the nitty-gritty part of the operation.

Have you set your departure date yet? If so, you can now tackle some of the paper work.

Your boat must be registered and have a certificate to prove it. To get a yacht registered through the Department of Trade and Industry takes a couple of months, costs nearly £50, and involves producing Bills of Sale for every change of ownership, plus a certificate of building from the builder. In the case of an old boat this mountain of paper may be almost impossible to obtain. A better way is to join the Royal Yachting Association and apply for their *Certificat de Registration,* which is acceptable virtually everywhere.

For yourself you need a valid passport with appropriate visas. At the time of writing none are required for any of the places mentioned, and also true at the time of writing is the fact that there is no need to produce any innoculation certificates. This is something you should bear in mind, however, in case epidemics create a situation where a certificate is required.

It might also be an idea to equip yourself with an Access Card or Barclaycard or some other means of trying to get instant credit.

The cruise through the French canals involves you in getting more essential pieces of paper. The first is the *Permis de Circulation,* which you get by applying to French Government Tourist Office, 178, Piccadilly, London, W.1. Allow a few weeks. This will be required no longer after June 26th 1974.

You require a *Passeport du Navire Etranger,* also known as a 'Green Card'. This is an obligatory requirement of the French Customs and you can get it either by writing to the *Ministere de l'Economie et des Finances, 71, Blvd. Periere, Paris, 17ème,* in advance, or by visiting the *Douane* at the first port of entry into France. You have to get the Green Card stamped at this port anyway, but taking it with you may save a little time.

The *Permis* has to be produced at intervals throughout the

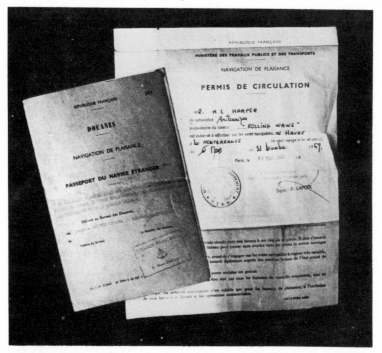

The two essential documents – the Permis de Circulation and the Passe-port du Navire Etranger. Yachts under 20 tons can pass without the skipper having to carry a certificate proving his capacity.

canals and to get it you must indicate the exact route you intend to follow. It is only valid for six months. The Green Card is essential to enable you to escape paying import duty for the first six months you are in French waters. It will also help you avoid paying the same duty on spares and parts (if you stick out for it). A photostat to leave with the agent will help. You need the original in your possession always.

In order to produce an itinerary you must have the list of *chômages.* This is a programme of the closures in the system throughout the year – the dates when specified canals and locks are closed for cleaning and maintenance, and if you don't work out your schedule bearing in mind its contents there is every chance that you will find yourself unable to move backwards or forwards for up to a month. Trapped! Let me out!

The list of *chômages* is obtainable from the French Tourist Office.

If you think that your stay may be prolonged beyond the six-month limit you should have words with the French customs officials to see if you can arrange to have the boat bonded. This can be arranged for a total of three six-month periods in three successive years, and is important to avoid paying the import duty. Contact: *Direction Generale des Douanes,* Centre de Renseignements Douaniers, 182, Rue St. Honore, 75, Paris 8 eme.

With your programme beginning to take shape you can produce a list of places where people can write to you and the dates you anticipate leaving. We found that the *poste restante* system works well though not infallibly providing you stick to your time-table and your correspondents allow plenty of time for letters to arrive at the post office.

If your list of places and times is too long you will find that you are making your plans too inflexible to allow for delays due to weather or engine trouble and so on, and you may find you are making trips you don't really want just to collect your mail.

This is also the time to start making the arrangements we discussed earlier like making your will and so on. It is the time to prune your standing order list with the bank because you probably won't have enough money coming in to cover the payments!

Check the boat over very thoroughly. Is the hull tight? What needs to be done to the engine? What gear needs to be replaced or added? Is the accommodation really comfortable, adequate for permanent living in for six months? Or what needs to be done to bring a tolerable degree of luxury into the boat? She is going to be your home for a long time and the minor discomforts which are tolerable for week-end cruising or two to three weeks at a time will be unacceptable after a month or so, especially in the heat of the Med.

This is particularly true of cooking arrangements. It may be worth investing in a new and larger cooker, one with an oven if the old one is lacking in this respect.

How about a fridge? In the hot weather you are going to be enjoying, a fridge is almost a necessity. Electrolux make a calor fridge which they sell for use in caravans, though they will not sell one knowingly into a boat. If the line from the gas cylinder is properly done there is little danger because the safety bi-metal valve will turn the gas supply off even if the flame blows out, and this is more than you can say for cookers!

Alternatively, there are fridges which run off the main battery either on 12 volts or 24 volts. These may well use so much current in hot climates that they will drain the battery very speedily, with the result that you are going to be the most unpopular guy on the mooring, the one with the generator popping away all night.

I have found the calor type perfectly satisfactory, and if the cooker runs off calor too there is an obvious advantage in making the fridge the same.

Your gas consumption will increase: we found a cylinder, the normal-sized 32lb one, would last about a month.

There are one or two misconceptions about calor gas. If the plumbing is a hundred per cent and if you always open the tap when the match is already there, and instruct any visitors to do the same, you should have no problems. If you are in doubt you can invest in one of the gas detector devices, which are not bad things to have anyway. There are several on the market, and Aquasonic Services make an automatic gas extractor.

We found that it was always possible to get a UK gas bottle filled on our travels. What happens is that you arrange with the local gas distributor to collect your empty cylinder, which he will return filled the next day. This is better than messing around with adaptors to try to overcome the problem created by a difference in threads between your regulator and the local bottle.

Socovam in Paris sell a cylinder which has the same thread as calor gas, but there is a hefty deposit on the bottle and the only way to get your money back is to return it to the place which supplied it originally and take the receipt with you. In practice this means that you lose your money!

So the best policy is to take two UK calor cylinders with you and make arrangements to get the empty one filled at the first opportunity.

Before you go you will want to tart up your boat as much as you can and anti-foul the bottom. The hot sun and warm water of the Med. combine to make weed grow on the bottom of a yacht at an incredible rate, especially along the water-line if you have it painted with boot-topping. An anti-fouling boot-topping is a good idea, and despite the incredible price of the paint itself, its covering rate is extremely good, and you will find that a little paint goes a very long way. So it is worth paying your money and feeling big.

Gribble and toredo don't seem to find a home on a boat which keeps on the move, so this is one problem which should not bother you too much.

You will probably find that no matter how good your intentions, you will have neither time nor energy to work on the paint while you are away. Just in case you behave to the contrary it is essential to take everything with you — paint, all colours and including primers, undercoatings and top-coats; masking tape; stopping; varnish; brushes, turps substitute; caulking cotton and oakum; sandpaper; stripping knives, the lot, because this kind of chandlery is very expensive and often hard to obtain in the Med.

As a matter of interest, we entered the harbour at Palma, Mallorca, with a fine growth of weed at least a foot long trailing from our water-line: within twenty-four hours it had turned to jelly and vanished. Just what effect the Palma water would have upon the fine human frame if one went swimming there doesn't bear dwelling upon!

If you can find or make space to stow it, a folding bicycle is a valuable asset to have with you. You may find yourself tied up somewhere miles from anywhere and the wine is running out! Folding bikes cost from £18 to £35 depending on where you shop and they aren't all that easy to stow, mainly because they are very difficult to handle when collapsed. So some very cunning carpentry may be required to provide a suitable nest.

It is not always easy to top up with drinking water, and not all water offered is fit to drink, even if it is described as 'potable'. Hence you may have to increase the water capacity in your boat. If you do this it is best to have separate tanks, one for water the quality of which is undoubted and which is therefore reserved for drinking purposes, and the other for water for washing and adding to whisky. If you take a couple of plastic 5-gallon jerricans with you, as I suggested earlier, to enable you to carry water when the tap is half a mile away, this will give you a reserve of ten gallons of water, providing you always keep them topped up when filling the tanks.

Our capacity on *Rolling Wave* is around 90 gallons including the jerricans, and with normal useage lasts two of us around three weeks. With the kind of economy practised by the round the world voyagers — half a gallon a day? — it would last about three months, but we don't count ourselves in that class.

Taps are very wasteful with water and should be replaced by pumps.

Just saying that water is not always potable even when so described is not good enough. Most water in France is fit to drink, unless it is well water. Take purifying tablets from the chemist just to be on the safe side. Water in Spain is suspect in most places other than large towns, because water is often collected in cisterns on roofs in wet weather and stored there until required later, by which time it is anything but pure. This water is not to be drunk even if the tablets are added. It is sometimes described as 'potable' even so!

There is a problem attached to canal-bashing which is seldom mentioned in the literature on the subject, and that is the fact that most of the journey will be done at very low engine speeds, so low that most engines will not be running fast enough to charge the battery. Hence there is a drain on the battery every time the engine is started, and juice taken from the battery when the lights are used is not replaced either. One possible answer is to replace your dynamo with the appropriate size of alternator. Another is to install some sort of charging set, and run the risk of driving everyone mad with the buzzing noise they all seem to make.

If you have a hand start engine the problem is not so acute, and the lighting problem can be solved by using paraffin or Camping Gaz lamps. This highlights the problem, of course, which is that the slow running and constant drain on the battery may finally drain so much that you will be unable to turn the engine over to start it.

A further possibility is to replace the pulley wheel on the dynamo with a smaller one so that it will rotate faster when the engine is ticking over, but this brings in the danger that it will be turning too fast later when it is running at normal speeds. So you will have to change the pulley over again. The belt will also have to be changed.

Needless to say, the engine needs to be thoroughly over-hauled before you go. Any dubious bearings should be replaced. The alignment of engine, shaft and gear-box should be checked and corrected if they are not true. Make sure the couplings are good. Particular attention should be paid to keyways, everything on the steering assembly, the dynamo, water pump, bilge pumps, fuel pumps, glands, all the things which are usually taken for granted until they pack up on you. Once you are away you depend very much on your own resources.

Another essential item of equipment you might overlook is a riding light. This is almost certain to be a paraffin light, which means that you are going to have to find a storage place for paraffin. You probably won't use very much, so a two-gallon can will be sufficient. The French for paraffin is *Petrole Kerdane* and if you remember this you won't follow my example and nearly buy two gallons of medicinal paraffin from a chemist in error.

What sort of tender do you carry? A tender is an essential piece of equipment for this cruise. Whatever you take must be strong, seaworthy and light. It must be easily stowed, easily carried, easily launched. It is an encumbrance in the canals if it is carried in davits over the stern because large craft following you into a lock may well run into it.

The most suitable tender is a good inflatable powered by a moderate outboard. Inflatables can be stowed with one chamber de-flated, thus occupying less space but still pro-viding adequate support for two people in an emergency. One person can easily launch a smaller one unaided. They can be rowed quite easily unless the wind is very strong and blows them about. A low powered outboard pushes them around quite happily. Left in the water over-night they don't keep you awake by banging into the hull. All in all, I favour inflatables providing that you get a good one. A bad one is dangerous. There is now a British Standard for inflatables, and the only ones which meet it at the time of writing are the Avon and the C-Craft. So select one of these. It is easy to get inflatables overhauled and made good for another year's service and if you already have one it is as well to get this done before you go.

An inflatable is easily carried, including its engine. This is a C-craft nine footer.

In hot weather you should release some air from the chambers to prevent its expansion straining the seams.

All the sailing gear should be checked out in the same way as the engine and anything which requires attention or seems likely to reach that condition while you are away should be put right before you go. Just as it is not always easy to get paint and so on in the Med. it is not easy to get things like sailmaker's palms, needles, twine, and codline, and while everyday things like rope, blocks, shackles and so on are widely available they are far more expensive — so the moral again is to take it all with you.

The hull will also have to be checked out, including the secure fastening of things like guard rails, staunchions, pulpits and pushpits and cleats, and all the standing and running rigging must be overhauled.

In the six months of your trip the boat will get more of a hammering than in six years of normal week-end cruising.

The ground tackle should be looked at with a very critical eye. Is the main anchor really heavy enough? Is the chain strong enough and have you a long enough scope? At least 30 fathoms is needed, and 45 would be better. How about the second anchor? Is that man enough? There may be times when you will want to lie to both, or use the lighter one as a kedge.

The best type of anchor is the C-Q-R, but it's no use relying on its great holding power to permit you to use a nylon warp instead of a chain, which is common practice in the Med. Apart from anything else you need the weight of chain to act as a spring in bad weather to prevent the upward pull of the boat from up-rooting the anchor.

In good weather it may be OK to lie on the second anchor and a nylon rope, but even then you should have a few fathoms of chain shackled to the anchor, so that you are lying to the chain as well as the anchor.

We have discussed the medicine chest before but only briefly. In addition to the normal things like aspirin and Burnol, you should take lots of sticking plaster, lots of bandages, including a couple of elastic bandages for sprains, ointments for insect bites, cream for repelling mosquitoes and cream for treating the bites of those which evade the barrier, (it is a good idea to try to rig some form of removable anti-mosquito netting which can cover portholes and doors to your sleeping quarters).

If you are a slave to any proprietary nostrum remember to stock up with six months supply, plus something for either extreme of bowel activity, hangover pills, and the water purifying pills already mentioned.

Salt tablets? Worth bearing in mind in view of the length of time you will be spending in the hot weather of the Med.

and the amount of sweat you may well expend in such unduly strenuous activities as fishing up fouled anchors, carrying calor gas cylinders and so on.

ACTION POINT. Now re-check your master list of everything that has to be done before you go.

ACTION POINT. Start working through your list.

2.   To Paris

The first alternative – up the Seine
The second alternative – entering the canals at Calais
Hints on canal-bashing

The canal system of Europe is complex, and there are very many ports at which a yachtsman can enter it. But for a British yacht with the Med. as its objective there are really only two places to enter and two possible routes, both of which meet at Paris, and it is these two routes we shall consider now.

The first possibility is to enter the Seine at Le Havre and follow it all the way to Paris: the second possibility is to enter the canals at Calais and follow them until you arrive at the same place.

TO PARIS VIA THE SEINE.

This is the way I went and it is such a beautiful river that I would choose the same route again. There are not so very many locks and these are all large ones which you pass through in company with the barges and providing you behave with circumspection they will create no problems.

If you enter the canals for the first time in your life there could be a worse baptism than this. We shall discuss the business of canal-bashing later in some depth.

First, some vital information. The Admiralty chart for the Baie de la Seine is 2146, Imray Laurie Norie & Wilson's chart is Y70., while the French firm of Blondel la Rougery S.A. of 7 Rue Saint-Lazare, Paris, 9 eme., publish 1012 which covers the same area. The admiralty chart should be sufficient, though the Imray chart is very useful for the passage up the river itself.

High water at Le Havre is one hour ten minutes before high water at Dover, and at Honfleur it is 24 minutes before Le Havre.

The Seine is a busy commercial river used by very many large commercial ships, some of which go into Le Havre, but don't be fooled, a lot go up river to Rouen, and you are going to be there with them.

The tides are fierce in the Seine itself and you must work them.

The entrance to the estuary is cluttered by banks, but they are all well marked, and you should have no problem providing you follow the chart.

Le Havre itself can be entered at any state of the tide, and by using the Tancarville Canal you can enter the Seine at Port de Tancarville, about fifteen miles up the river, at just the right time to carry the whole of the flood.

There is an alternative to this scheme, which is to make your arrival on the Seine at the pretty little harbour of Honfleur which is located on the other side of the estuary just about opposite Le Havre.

If you do stop off at Honfleur you are a few miles nearer Tancarville than if you spend the night at Le Havre, but there is a complication regarding working the tides.

The outer harbour dries out completely, and it is not a harbour in which even a bilge keeler would want to stop, so you must lock into the inner basin. As a result of this you can only leave the inner basin when the flood has already run most of its course and you will therefore have only a short time with a favourable tide.

The lock is opened from about an hour before high water until about half an hour after, but the bridge which crosses the lock is normally only opened three times — an hour before high water, at high water, and finally, at high water plus half an hour. In fact, it is only twitched open for a fleeting moment, or so it seems, so you have to be ready and waiting to pass through, engine running and warps cast off. The lock-keeper-cum-bridge-opener seems to be paid a bonus for all the hours the bridge is open to traffic, and will have no compunction about closing it in your face.

The other problem which calling in at Honfleur entails is the ease with which you can be set past the entrance to the harbour and then be unable to make against the flood back again. The tides can run at speeds up to eight knots, so keep a sharp lookout. It is not a catastrophe if you do miss the entrance, because you can carry the tide and then anchor or moor up, but it will be a pity if you lose the opportunity to see Honfleur as a result.

If you are really in a hurry it is probably better to go into Le Havre and use the Tancarville Canal.

The estuary of the Seine is marked by a lightship which is moored roughly nine miles approximately west of Cap de la

You can sometimes hitch a lift with a barge.
(picture: Jonathan Eastland)

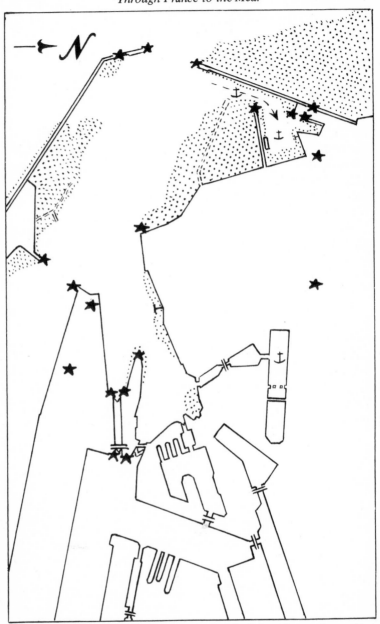

Le Havre. The yacht moorings are marked by the anchors. Stars represent lights.

Heve, though it may be replaced in the summer months by a buoy. The channels are well buoyed, but there are times when one may be masked by an anchored ship, which can be confusing.

Yachts are obliged to give way to commercial craft of sixty feet or over in the whole of the Le Havre/Seine area.

The harbour at Le Havre is enclosed by two long walls, both of which have conspicuous lights, and the yacht harbour is reached by turning hard to port immediately you are inside the entrance. If you cannot find a berth immediately on the pontoons tie up temporarily on the floating pontoon and seek help. If you intend to stay for long you can lock into the Bassin du Commerce at high water.

Access to the Tancarville Canal is gained by passing through the lock into the Bassin de L'Eure, which lies behind the Thorensen car ferry terminal, then through the Bassin Fluvial and Bassin Vétillart. The canal is fourteen miles long and has a lock at each end; the further one is only open around high water also, being linked intimately to the tidal streams of the river.

If you elect to go into Honfleur you follow the big ship channel, and take great care not to get involved with the long training wall named the Digue du Ratier. This is marked at the seaward end by a black dolphin, and the wall projects a long way out to sea. Keep well over to the proper side of the channel to give plenty of room to the commercial shipping.

The Digue is marked by beacons. A little after it becomes a solid masonry wall there is a gap which is the entrance to Honfleur. Don't hesitate, go straight in, because the current will set you past otherwise.

It is best to arrive a little before an hour before high water so that you can be all ready to enter when the lock and the bridge open.

The entrance channel is straight and forks after a short distance. Turn to starboard, pass the small basin and into the lock entrance itself, immediately in front of the bridge. Tie up to the wall in front of the gates where there will probably be a couple of fishing boats also waiting to go in.

Once inside the basin you tie up to one of the pontoons to port, if there is room, or against the wall to starboard.

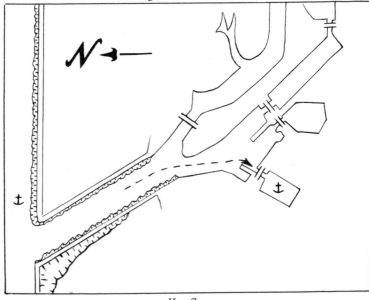

Honfleur

Honfleur is a smashing little town, full of mediaeval buildings, a launderette, which may be of more immediate interest, and a cathedral which is constructed of wood, and was built by ship wrights, a fact which is fairly evident from its design. Clinker or carvel? — go and see for yourself!

Back to the Seine itself. It is sometimes visited by a tidal bore, known locally as Le Mascaret. This sweeps upstream at the beginning of the flood during exceptional spring tides, and the effect is noticed as far as Caudebec and beyond. It is at its strongest between Caudebec and Quilleboeuf. It can be very dangerous for a yacht, especially a small one at moorings, when it may be lying with the ebb and suddenly be attacked from astern by the bore.

The maximum height of the bore is eight feet, but only when the exceptional spring tides coincide with the river in flood and a strong easterly wind blowing down river.

By working the tides, however, it is unlikely that you will be in the reaches of the river which are affected by Le Mascaret. Study of the tidal tables and a conversation with a fisherman or lock-keeper will keep you on the straight and narrow.

Your immediate objective once you are in the Seine is to get past Rouen, because after this the navigational problems are far less acute.

More facts: at Tancarville the flood can run at six knots and the ebb at four knots; above La Mailleraye the flood and the ebb both run at two to three knots. It is 55 miles from Tancarville to Rouen, where there is a prolonged high water stand, so that a yacht averaging five knots through the water and on the receiving end of the flood stream all the way from Tancarville should be able to carry her tide all the way.

Rouen itself is a thriving industrial town, is the third largest seaport in France, and is not everyone's idea of a good place to spend a nice quiet peaceful night. Some people, however claim to know of secret little moorings for the night where there is nothing to disturb.

A favourite place to moor is just below the fuelling point on the west side of the island just above the second bridge. Another place to try is the Bassin St. Gervais.

One of the refineries at Rouen. Not an ideal place to moor for the night.
(picture: Jonathan Eastland)

It is difficult to remember that Joan of Arc was burnt in Rouen in 1431: it gives the impression of having been an industrial town ever since the Ice Age!

If you have a mast you will be unable to pass under the bridges of Rouen. What do you do? The best thing probably is to do a deal with a crane driver at Le Havre. There was a small crane at the yacht club in Rouen at one time, but the story now is that the yacht club has moved away.

It is probably best to strike the mast at Le Havre anyway, because nothing is worse than suddenly being confronted by a bridge when you have the tide under you. The other alternative is to stop for a night a little short of Rouen and then proceed cautiously in the morning until you find a wharf which looks promising and negotiate your deal over the striking of the mast there.

There are a number of yacht clubs between Le Havre and Rouen, some with their own mooring buoys, and you may be able to arrange to tie up to one for a night. Or you may be able to anchor.

But it is best to try to get past Rouen as soon as you can to avoid being in the same reaches as the large ocean-going ships, even though there are still plenty of really big barges and small coasters all the way to Paris. Once you get past Rouen the effects of the tide are so much less that they can be largely ignored.

All this should be borne in mind if you plan your passage from Honfleur. Your inability to get out of the inner basin until an hour before high water means that you lose the benefit of the flood very quickly. One possibility is to carry the last of the flood from Honfleur to Tancarville and pick up a mooring buoy there for the night. Next day you will be able to carry the whole of the flood tide.

It is easy to identify Tancarville because of its vast suspension bridge, so large that the ocean-going ships which go to Rouen can pass under it easily. It is the largest suspension bridge in Europe.

Keep in the channel on the way to Tancarville. It is marked to port by light buoys and to starboard by beacons running along the Digue. A training wall continues to port even after the light buoys stop.

The bridge at Tancarville.

Above Tancarville the Seine runs through beautiful country, wooded and rolling, and the traffic is not so heavy that you will be prevented from appreciating it.

We found a very pleasant anchorage at a place called Chateau de la Cheminee Tournante, before the first lock at Amfreville. All was quiet, all was still, and the first spring freshness brought a pristine beauty to the scene. However, don't be fooled, the river is still tidal, with a rise and fall of some feet. There should be at least nine feet at low water springs, with less close in to the banks. Exceptional spring tides or heavy rainfall can upset all calculations.

The distance to the first lock at Amfreville from Rouen is twenty-five miles.

The Seine above Amfreville

There are the following locks between Rouen and Paris, not all of which will necessarily be in use:

Amfreville	3 chambers, 2 in use	25½ miles to
Notre Dame de la Garenne	2 chambers, 2 in use	10½ miles to

Port Villez	2 chambers, 2 in use	15 miles to
de Méricourt	2 chambers, 2 in use	16 miles to
des Mureaux	2 chambers, 2 in use	11 miles to
de Carriere sous Poissy	2 chambers, 2 in use	17 miles to
Bougival	3 chambers, 3 in use	20 miles to
Suresnes	3 chambers, 3 in use	10 miles to Port de Plaisance, Paris.

Barge traffic is very heavy all the way to Paris. Barges come in what seem to be standard sizes, to fit the dimensions of the different canals. The biggest, and quite awe-inspiring, are the pusher trains. These consist of very powerful pusher tugs, with up to six enormous lighters in front, which travel 24 hours a day, seven days a week, and nothing seems to stop them, fog, snow or worse. They navigate by radar when they

Leaving the locks at Amfreville. These two vast floating car parks are lighters and the cabin in the air at the left of the picture is the control tower of the pusher tu which will take them down the river.
(picture: Jonathan Eastland)

can't see, and two families live on board to provide the crew to enable them to be manned continuously.

These pusher tugs have very powerful engines and should be given a very wide berth at all times, and not just because of their sheer size and the problems they have in manoeuvring. I made the mistake once of lingering behind one when it was waiting to enter a lock. When it put its engines in gear and turned the taps on the wash was so great that I very nearly found myself blasted up the river bank.

In general the rule is to keep to the starboard hand in the river. Sometimes a deep laden barge will fly a blue flag from the side of his wheelhouse to indicate that he is unable to follow the rules because of his deep draught or the throw of his screw. Sound signals may augment the flags — a long and a short indicates 'pass to the right'; a long and two shorts indicates pass to the left. The acknowledgement signal is either one short or two shorts.

If the current is strong enough to be significant the vessel carrying it has right of way, which is particularly important at bridges. If two vessels are likely to meet head-on at a curve the one with the outside of the bend on her starboard hand has right of way.

A vessel with greater speed may overtake, but not within 500 metres — a little over 500 yards — of a lock. A vessel may not overtake on a blind corner or when approaching a bridge.

A very long blast followed by one short one means 'I am going to overtake you on the right', while a very long blast followed by two short ones means 'I am going to overtake you to port'. The vessel being overtaken must keep to the proper side of the channel and maintain or reduce her speed and acknowledge by sounding one or two short blasts, whichever is appropriate.

Four short blasts signifies that a vessel should not be overtaken.

A barge which has the current under her and intends to turn into it will sound two prolonged blasts followed by one short if she intends to turn to starboard and two if she means to go to port. While she is actually turning she has right of way.

The signal to attract a lock-keeper's attention to the fact

that you wish to enter the lock is one prolonged blast, but there are times when it may be tactless to make this signal! If you have to wait while a lock is emptied for you it is often better to stooge about rather than tie up, providing that you don't get in other people's way.

It is your own responsibility to make yourself fast in a lock and not the lock-keepers, though he will often help you, especially as you may sometimes have great difficulty in reaching a bollard or getting ashore. It is therefore your problem to enter in such a way that you can put a member of the crew ashore. Oh those ladders!

Conversely it is your responsibility to cast off your warps and retrieve your crew when you leave a lock.

In the large locks on the Seine you are certain to be passing through in company with barges. It is thus best to try to be the last to enter – and don't keep them waiting! – and then make fast to a barge.

The lock-keepers have absolute authority in their locks, including determining who has priority in entering. Most of them are very helpful and co-operative, and they appreciate courtesy from a yachtsman. Unfortunately they don't always get it and if you acquire a reputation as a pig the jungle telegraph which connects locks will operate to ensure that your evil name will precede you.

The barge people are very pleasant too, and they react very favourably to a little courtesy. They work very long hours in a job which calls for considerable skill and knowledge and their help and advice is always well worth seeking.

If you should get up a barge skipper's hooter it pays to remember that he has a large and invincible weapon with which to retaliate in the sheer bulk of his barge!

You will often find yourself in company with the same barge at two or three successive locks, and a few words will usually elicit useful information – like a good place to tie up for the night. What could be better than alongside a barge with a friendly skipper!

Even the small barges create a considerable wash with their propellers when they leave a lock, so it pays not to get close behind them and to keep your warps tight until they are clear.

Chateau Guillard, near Les Andeleys. This is the ruin of the home of Richard the Lionheart.
(picture: Jonathan Eastland)

Always keep a good tension on your warps in a lock because eddies and whirlpools are created when the sluices are opened and a yacht can easily be thrown about. The disturbance is less at the back of a lock than at the front, another reason for tucking yourself in last.

The locks on the Seine are all large and the real problem is to get through and not be by-passed by all the barges. Many of the locks have loudhailers and they will tell you if they want you to enter. It is usually impossible to understand the kind of fractured French these systems produce, but if you can recognise the magic words *'bateau Anglais'* the chances are that they are calling for you. Don't hang around, they won't keep the barges waiting longer than they must, and if you dither they will shut the gates in your face.

Closed circuit TV is used in many Seine locks so that the lock-keeper can see what is happening from his concrete eyrie high above the basin.

Often a barge skipper will translate the loudhailer instructions for you into slightly more comprehensible French if he sees that you are baffled.

At the time I thought that negotiating the Seine locks was hard work, and so it was. With the benefit of the advice given here you should have an easier ride. But I still have happy memories of the barge families gossiping to each other in the locks, and of barges full of sand castles with chickens scratching about on them and the triumphant cackling of a hen which has just laid an egg rising incongruously above the thump of the barge's diesel engines.

If you get an opportunity, stop and explore the village of Conflans St Honorine, which lies between Ecluse de Carriere sous Poissy and Ecluse de Bougival. This is the centre of the in-world of the barge people, and even has a church built on a barge hull in which weddings between the barging families are celebrated.

TO PARIS FROM CALAIS

The route takes you to Watten up the Canal du Calais and the river Aa, then on to Chauny along the Canal de Neuffosse, then along the Canal d'Aire, Canal de la Deule, Canal de la Sensée, the river Escaut and the Canal de Saint-Quentin.

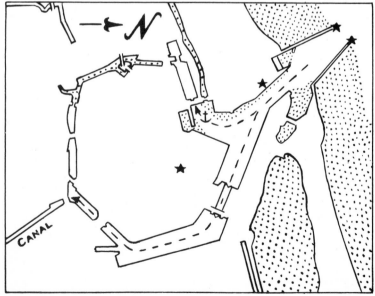

Calais. The anchor indicates the entrance to the yacht basin and the dashed line shows the way into the canal.

Inside the yacht basin at Calais, where you may decide to wait before entering the canal. Berthing is cheaper on the wall opposite.

From Chauny you follow the Canal Latéral a l'Oise and the river Oise to Conflans St. Honorine.

Calais can be entered at any state of the tide. The canal to Watten is reached by passing through the Ecluse Carnot, and if you have to wait to lock in, a convenient place to tie up is the wall which runs at right angles to the quay used by the cross-Channel ferries. This is the wall which yachts normally use to wait when they arrive too early to lock straight into the yacht-club basin.

The Ecluse Carnot is a large one, which lies just past the cross-Channel ferry jetty. It opens from two hours before high water to one hour after, and is used by a considerable volume of commercial traffic.

The canal runs for nineteen miles before it reaches the Aa, and there is only one lock, which is located at a place called Ste-Marie-Kerque, and the lock itself only lifts you about three feet. The canal has at least seven feet of water in it and the air height is at least 11ft 9ins. Three and three quarters of a mile past the lock you turn to starboard at a swing bridge, Pont-du-West, into the river Aa. Ignore the three branches of the other canals which enter the canal on the right at various places along the route.

The Aa is five-and-a-half miles long and has one lock, called Ecluse de Haut Pont. At St.Omer the river joins the Canal de Neuffosse, a good place to stop for the night.

Just past St. Omer you pass through another lock, the Ecluse de Flandres, and at La Fontinette, a little more than a mile further on, there is a hydraulic lift which raises you more than 43ft. As an alternative to be used when the lift is out of action, as it may be for maintenance, there is the five-lock staircase which the lift replaces.

The canal meets the Canal d'Aire at Aire-sur-la-Lys, and some twenty-five miles further on this in turn meets the Canal de la Deule at Bauvin. There is one lock with two chambers on the Canal d'Aire, about nineteen miles from Aire-sur-la-Lys.

The Canal d'Aire runs through pleasant countryside, dotted with market towns such as Bethune and La Bassee, where troops resting during the Great War swam in the canal during their rest periods out of the line.

Bauvin is some ten miles after the lock, and here you turn to starboard into the very busy Canal de la Deule. This canal connects the river Scarpe with the river Lys, and is really the river Deule canalised. It carries heavy commercial traffic between the North Sea waterways and the Parisian and southern canal systems of France. This section of the Canal de la Deule contains no locks.

After fourteen miles the canal by-passes the busy town of Douai — take the starboard fork — and runs into the Canal de Derivation de la Scarpe, which in turn meets the Canal de la Sensée at Corbeheim.

This canal is only fifteen miles long, and has one lock two-and-a-half miles from its junction with the Canal de Derivation de la Scarpe, another very busy waterway with heavy commercial traffic. Ignore the junction with the Canal du Nord, which lies to starboard after five-and-a-half miles, and turn to starboard into the river Escaut at Bassin-Rond.

The Escaut is another short river, only eight miles long, but it too bears heavy traffic, and there are four large locks to pass through, each with twin chambers. The canalised river enters the Canal de Saint-Quentin at Cambrai. After 56 miles and after negotiating 36 locks it meets the Canal Latéral a l'Oise at Chauny. This canal runs through summit tunnels which cost about £5 in toll fees, and there are special arrangements to pass through them. You should seek the advice of barge skippers to ensure you have the latest information.

The first of these tunnels is called le Bony, and it is a fascinating speculation that it is possible that its name is derived from the fact that it was constructed between 1802 and 1810 by prisoners of war of the great Napoleon.

Normally there are convoys in each direction at certain times each day, and the barges are towed through with yachts last in line. It takes some time to negotiate the first tunnel, and night convoys stop for a few hours in a basin for a rest and to enable a convoy heading in the opposite direction to pass. The same thing happens in the day-time, except that the string of barges pauses for a shorter time.

The second tunnel, named de Lesdins, sometimes known as du Tronquoy, is shorter, only about ¾ mile, but this is taken in convoy too.

The usual departure times of the convoys are 1pm or 10pm.

The passage through these tunnels can be unnerving for any one who suffers from claustrophobia, especially if you find yourself in the night convoy which stops for several hours. The impression is that of being in a tomb, and it can be quite shattering.

On this last run into Chauny you pass two other junctions with other canals. There is a turning to starboard, after the Ecluse de Port-Tugay, which is the Canal de la Somme, and to port after the Ecluse de Fargniers there is a branch canal to La Fere.

At Chauny you enter the Canal Latéral a l'Oise, leading into the river Oise and then at Janville you finally make your way into the river Seine at Conflans St. Honorine. The commercial traffic continues to be heavy all the way. There are eleven locks and it is 21 miles from Chauny to Janville, 65 miles from Janville to Conflans-St. Honorine. The commercial traffic continues to be heavy all the way. There are eleven locks and it is twenty-one miles from Chauny to Janville, sixty-five miles from Janville to Conflans-St. Honorine.

If you are blessed with a sense of history you should find many opportunities all along this route to indulge yourself. Apart from Cambrai, famous for its participation in two world wars as well as being the place where cambric cloth originated, you pass through Compiègne, where Foch received the German surrender in 1918 and where Hitler reversed the situation by accepting the French surrender in 1940.

PARIS

The Port de Plaisance in Paris provides the kind of amenities which are so sadly lacking in London. It is located right in the heart of the city, a few minutes' walk from the Champs Elysée, hard by the Place de la Concorde. The *Touring Club de France* is the controlling body, and their houseboat headquarters is tied up on the port side immediately after the Pont Alexandre III. The moorings extend for a considerable distance, from Pont Invalides to Pont de la Concorde.

There is a tremendous amount of river traffic through Paris, not only barges, but the large fast boats which take tourists up and down the river. The result of this traffic is a heavy and continuing swell, which means that you must make very sure that your warps are adequate. In addition the traffic never seems to stop tearing round the Place de la Concorde, and the noise is so constant that one feels eventually that one is moored in the middle of Hyde Park Corner.

The wear and tear from these two sources is so great that you are unlikely to get any sleep at all while you are moored here. Indeed, you may well decide to cut short your stay in Paris.

Nevertheless, Paris is the place to stop to enable you to gird up your loins, as it were, for the canals and the locks which lie ahead.

While you are here, with all the Parisian facilities at your disposal, you should check-out the engine, top up with fuel and lubricating oil, fill the tanks with water, charge up your battery and collect your mail. Don't forget to leave a forwarding address. By now you may have found that there are one or two items of equipment which you need and it is better to buy them now because once in the canals it may be

This statue marks the official limit of the port of Paris.
(picture: Jonathan Eastland)

impossible to find a shop or a chandler, and prices are steep in the Med.

This business of charging up batteries is particularly important because, as we have already seen, the slow speeds enforced on you in the canals will result in your batteries becoming flat, unless you have taken the precautions already discussed.

MORE ABOUT CANAL BASHING

By the time you reach Paris you will have had quite a baptism of working locks, but whether you selected the route straight down the Seine or the web of canals from Calais, your experience will have all been on busy locks in busy waterways, with heavy barge traffic, and all the locks will have been large ones, electrically operated, where you just go in with the barges.

But on the Marne and the subsequent canals it is very different. There are fewer barges and you will find that most

When the gates open in the large locks the barges fight each other to be the first away. The middle one has priority.
(picture: Jonathan Eastland)

of the locks are small ones which you are expected to assist in operating.

Some of these locks are oval, some are rectangular, some have sloping sides. The thing to do is to establish some kind of drill which will enable you to take them in your stride.

In the larger locks there are the same dangers as on the Seine of getting crushed or crunched by a barge, and there is the added need to take care not to get swept into the weir stream if you elect to dither about while waiting for the lock gates to open, rather than tie up. There is also a possibility of going aground outside some of the locks if you stray from the obvious approach channel. Most of these hazards are well sign-posted.

There are only a few of the locks with sloping sides. The problem here is to make sure that you are properly tied up when the sluices are opened. There is no bollard on the edge of the lock to which you make fast, and it is impossible to clamber up the sloping wall to get to the top anyway. The answer is to take a stern line to the bollard on the knuckle as you enter the chamber.

In the rectangular locks you will sometimes find that you will be able to lie safely to just a breast rope even if the sluices are opened before you have bow and stern lines ashore. It is best to keep the engine running in these locks in the same way as the barges do.

On the canals there is no room for a yacht in the locks as well as a barge. The barges are built to fit exactly. But if you can team up with another yacht, and proceed in convoy with her, the amount of work involved in passing through the locks will be halved.

In the smaller locks the lock-keeper opens the gates and then works the sluices on the side of the lock on which his house stands while you operate the sluices and the gates on the other. As you approach the lock you have to note which side the towpath follows and which side the house is on. This will dictate the position of the ladder up which your crew will have to climb, and the position of the ladder down which he will have to scramble as you leave the lock. The ladder is almost invariably opposite the lock-keeper's side.

A frequent sight in the canals is women scrubbing clothes

in specially built wash-houses at the canal's edge. Remember what effect your wash will have upon them if you pass at too great a speed.

Passing an oncoming barge in the canals can also create problems. The volume of water displaced by the barge is so great and the clearance round it in restricted canals so little that the result is a great hump of water being pushed in front of the barge, which will thrust a yacht bodily to one side. If the barge is deeply laden there will be insufficient water along the canal bank for him to draw to one side to give you room. Hence you will have to slow down, move over as far as you can, and then increase engine revolutions when his bow wave reaches you. With good steerage way it is easy then to keep from being swept aside and to steer through his wash back into the middle of the channel again. The water is sucked away from the bank as the barge passes so that you will bump if you are too close in. The canals are constantly being dredged. Watch out for the dredger's mooring warps. The

This picture shows clearly just how the barges push a hill of water ahead of them in the canals.

'passing side' is indicated by a green circle with a white centre, while the non-passing side is marked by a red circle with a white centre. A red flag on a barge indicates that the side which carries it is his wrong side and that you should pass on the other side.

On the Seine we found there were no problems in over-taking because the river was so wide and the only things to watch out for were bridges, other craft, and dredgers. But in the canals there is so little room that over-taking or being over-taken creates difficulties. Often it is not possible at all, and if you get stuck behind a barge you will have the frustration of approaching every lock and finding the gates closed and the water level wrong. It is better to stop and have a coffee than attempt to pass when it is dangerous to do so. If you do manage to squeeze past the barge he will then be the one with the gates against him, and the old canal grape-vine will then operate – probably by telephone – so that your reception may not be good from then on.

One thing which the canals have in common with the Seine is that it is not always easy to find somewhere to tie up for the night. There is not always very much water along the banks, and if the level drops in the night you may find your-self aground in the morning. This is where your scaffold boards may come in useful to act as props to keep you off.

3.   Down to the Med.

To Chalons-sur-Saône
To Port St.Louis

THE ALTERNATIVES

From Paris there are three possible routes to the Med. but
they all take you through Chalons-sur-Sâone and on to
Lyons, where you pick up the Rhône pilot and in two days
can be in that beautiful clear blue water you have been
dreaming about.

The possibilities are:-

via the Marne	450 miles	166 locks to Lyons
via Burgandy	394 miles	228 locks to Lyons
via the Bourbonnais	396 miles	167 locks to Lyons

The complication of the Burgandy route is that there is
little air height under the bridges – 9ft 10ins. at the centre
compared with 11ft 6ins. for the Bourbonnais and 11ft 9ins.
for the Marne. The length and width of the locks is the same
for all three routes and so is the least depth of water. The
extra number of locks on the Burgandy system also more
than outweighs the slightly shorter distance.

So the choice really lies between the Marne and the Bourbonnais. There is a tunnel on the Canal du Bourgogne with an
air height of 10ft 1in. at the centre and a rather rounded
cross section, which has to be negotiated under tow, while on
the Canal de la Marne a la Saône there is a tunnel with an air
height of 18ft 7ins. which is taken in convoy but under your
own power.

Hence I favour the Marne route. The extra mileage represents — what, one day, two days? on the trip, and by spreading the locks over another couple of days the chore of lock-bashing is lessened. The tunnel on the Marne is a better proposition too. So in this book the Marne route only is described. Besides, following this system takes you through some first class wine country, including Champagne!

THE MARNE

As I have already said, the pleasures of Paris are likely to pass fairly rapidly thanks to the discomforts of the Port de Plaisance, so it's heigh ho! and off to the Marne.

The entrance to the river is on the port hand only a few miles from the Port de Plaisance, at Charenton, a little over half a mile past Pont de Conflans and just before the Pont d'Ivry sur Seine.

Passing under the bridges of Paris presents no aggravation providing you stick to the channel, which is well marked. You could always take up position astern of a barge and follow in his wake.

The Marne has 18 locks and you follow it for 117 miles,

Pont Alexandre Trois in Paris.
(picture: Jonathan Eastland)

when it leads you into the Canal Latéral a la Marne at Dizy, through a lock which it is very easy to miss because the gate is not marked and resembles a wall rather than a lock gate.

Much of the Marne is reminiscent of the Thames. You see skiffs, dinghy races, pleasure steamers and regattas, and officials are likely to chase you at a very rapid rate in order to instruct you to slow down and make less wash. The scenery is attractive, often like the Thames, complete with similar tycoon's week-end cottages overlooking the water.

The first two locks are close together, and a short tunnel follows closely after the second lock. It has 15ft. 3ins. in the centre and traffic signals control movement through it. Red alone means stop, green alone means pass, red and green horizontally means prepare to enter. The tunnel is six hundred metres long and its purpose is to by-pass the river.

The next stretch of river is crossed by very many bridges and is dotted with islands. The pleasure boat traffic can be heavy and so can the barge traffic. Watch closely for the signs indicating the channel.

The next lock, Ecluse de Neuilly-sur-la-Marne, leads into another canal diversion from the main river, and after four and a half miles you re-enter it by the Ecluse de Vaires. Another six miles brings you into a busy little stretch, and the Ecluse de Chalifert is followed immediately by another tunnel, a short one this time, of 656 yards with nearly 17ft headroom. There are no signals to tell you whether or not you may pass, but the lock-keeper will give you instructions.

This tunnel is followed immediately by another lock, Ecluse de Lesches, and parts of the channel in this area have silted up. If possible follow a barge, stay in the channel, and don't wander. This isn't the best place to go aground.

You are now in another deviation from the Marne itself, and you re-enter it seven and a half miles later through the Ecluse de Meaux. Here again the channel wanders, and you must keep to it. About a mile and a quarter before the next lock, Ecluse d'Isles-les-Meldeuses, which lies immediately after a conspicuous road bridge, the channel swerves abruptly to starboard round a flooded island.

The following lock is the Ecluse de Saint Jean, eight miles on, and the channel changes from one side of the river to the

other, followed a further eight miles later by Ecluse Court-
aron. After another five problem-free miles you reach Ecluse
Mèry, Ecluse Charly after five and a half miles and Ecluse
d'Azy after six.

There are shallows in the vicinity of this last lock and
rocks just below the water along the bank in front of the lock
itself and therefore not a good place to go alongside to wait
for the lock to open. The hazard is marked.

The river meanders on, passing through the small town of
Chateau-Thierry, scene of much fighting in both world wars,
and after nine miles you reach the next lock, Ecluse de Mont
St Pere. You must be careful to stay in the channel after this
one, and then after seven and a half miles you reach Ecluse
de Courelle.

By now the barge traffic will have thinned out very considerably, and if you are beginning to get a little tired of
locks and canals reflect on the fact that you have an awful lot
more locks to come, but that the passage becomes pro-
gressively easier. And what are 150 odd locks anyway?

There is a strip chart for the Marne, obtainable from
Editions Maritimes et d'Outre-Mer, 17 Rue Jacob, Paris VI
and on it somewhere one reads what in Harper style French
translates as 'Le Tour de Marne offers little of interest to the
nautical tourist. Lighter boats are susceptible to being swiftly
transported across and under the weirs. In general, parts of
the Marne, outside the navigation canals, require delicate
navigation and demand a real experience of the river. In
several sections only hand locks are employed and numerous
difficulties arise due to shortage of water. . .' Yes, well, there
may be some truth in all that. . . .

The business about shortage of water is true. You may find
that the level has dropped in the night and that instead of
just being afloat you are now just aground and will be unable
to get off until the level rises again. The mud along the banks
is usually soft, so it is worth trying to pole off with engine
going full bore if this should happen to you.

Many of the locks have terrifying weirs, so they should be
approached with circumspection. After Ecluse de Courelle
you travel for eight miles to Ecluse de Vandieres, and still the
channel runs between islands and you have to take care to

keep in it. This lock is the first one with sloping sides, and you take your stern line to a bollard on the knuckle as you enter. When the sluices are open the water just rushes in like a waterfall and you are unlikely to be given much time in which to get settled.

The next lock, Ecluse de Damery, also has sloping sides, and leads into another diversion from the river itself, a short run of five and a half miles to Ecluse de Cumieres, the last sloping-sided lock.

It is now a short run, just over two miles, until you enter the Canal Latéral a la Marne through the Ecluse de Dizy, which is a normal square-sided lock.

CANAL LATERAL A LA MARNE
This is a fairly short canal, with a length of 41½ miles and a total of only 15 locks. It enters the Canal de la Marne a la Saône at Vitry-le-Francois, well into the champagne country. Epernay, the centre for the production of champagne, lies down the Marne itself, about two miles from the canal, and if you are ahead of schedule you could do worse than make a detour down the river to the famous cellars before you actually enter the canal.

From now on the canals and the locks are much easier to negotiate. There is more physical work on your part, because you will have to do half the work of opening the locks, operating the sluices, and opening the gates when you are ready to leave them.

The Canal Latéral a la Marne and the Canal de la Marne a la Saône take you through the rural heart of France. You may be surprised, as I was, to motor slowly through villages where the canal runs like a road separating the right side of the village from the wrong and chickens run in and out of the houses. Where the lock-keepers have time to stop and talk and are anxious to do so, and where the French they use has less resemblance to the alleged Parisian French we were taught at school than it has to Mandarin. Where bicycles appear to be the normal form of transport.

The canal gradually ascends, and the vegetation changes slowly as it does so. Finally you are passing through conifers and the lock-keepers' houses seem to be the only ones for miles.

The change into the Canal de la Marne a la Saône is imperceptible at Vitry-le-Francois, a town of 15,000 people, where the Canal de la Marne au Rhin converges also. Finally you reach the summit level tunnel at Balesmes, which we will talk about at more length in a minute.

The Canal de la Marne a la Saône has 114 locks and is 139 miles long. There are two tunnels, the short one at Conde which is only 337 yards long and is subject to no special controls, and the long one at Balesmes.

There is comparatively little barge traffic now, all the locks are hand operated and there is no problem of hazardous weirs. Apart from the sheer grind of working the locks the trip is easy. It might be a good idea to stop for a day once you get past Dizy and do nothing except relax.

CANAL DE LA MARNE A LA SAONE
The tunnel at Balesmes is towards the end of the canal, after you have passed through the small town of Langres, which has a beautiful 12th century cathedral.

It is about three miles long and special regulations govern its passage. Traffic is one way only and there are time schedules governing the times the convoys depart from each end. You go under your own power, normally leaving the northern end at midnight or some time between noon and the late afternoon. The trip takes about two hours.

What happens is that a convoy gathers and all go through together, nose to tail. If you arrive when there is no barge waiting it is best to tie up until one arrives and check with the skipper about the times of the convoys. There is one-way traffic for about two miles before the tunnel.

You will need a good powerful torch to pass through because there is no artificial light at all, and you just follow the glow-worm which is the stern light of the vessel in front. Without a torch it is almost impossible to avoid bashing into the sides of the tunnel or over-running the vessel ahead. Width is 19ft 6ins. and headroom is 18ft 6ins.

I was rather intrigued when I passed through to see the skipper of the barge ahead leap ashore a few hundred yards short of the tunnel mouth, carefully select a branch of a tree which he then trimmed of its branches. Its purpose became

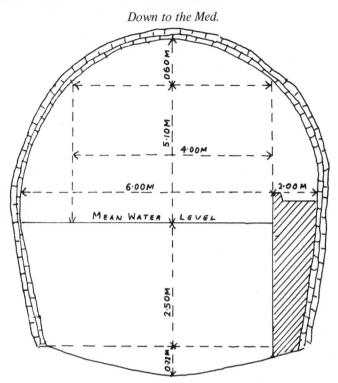

Cross section of the tunnel at Balesmes.

clear once in the tunnel — it acted as a guide and a fender between the side of the barge and the side of the tunnel. The bargeman's technique seemed to be to run the barge along the tunnel side and the branch protected the hull from chafe.

There should be no need for a yachtsman to have to follow this example!

The height of this tunnel is no less than 1,115 feet above sea level, a fact upon which to reflect as you wind all those handles at the locks.

The first eight locks after the tunnel all come on top of each other and they only take one barge at a time, so there is a natural build up of traffic from the convoy and you may have to wait for your turn. It is best to get well clear of these first eight locks before you tie up for the night.

My wife and I had a big debate after the first pair of locks — was it possible that the lock-keeper of the second lock was the twin brother of the lock-keeper of the first? The mystery was solved when we left the second lock and watched the man get on his bike and roar back up the hill to the first of his charges.

There are 71 locks before the tunnel and 43 after. You will have already done eight of these, so you have only 35 to go, then you enter the river Saône at Heuilley.

It seems a little strange at first to be going into locks which are full instead of locks which are empty, and it calls for a slightly different drill, but after a very few you will find you can do it in your sleep.

One of the smaller dredgers which are a common sight in the canals. Their mooring wires are a real hazard as they often straddle the width of the canal. (picture: Hugh McKnight)

LA SAONE

After the placid waters of the canals it is a shock to realise that once again you are on a waterway which is encumbered by sandbanks and bars, which has a current which can increase quite alarmingly if the river floods after heavy rain, and another hazard, the '*cléonages*', the training walls which are built up to direct the current and encourage it to scour out the main channels. Like the Marne there are sections where the river has been canalised or by-passed by sections of canal.

The biggest hazard of these is the *cléonages.* The tops are usually just at the level of the surface of the river or just below it. It is vital therefore to keep in the marked channel and to obey all navigational signs.

There is a considerable amount of dredging on the Saône, as indeed there is throughout the canal system, but on the Saône it is more intensive – and more necessary.

There are twelve locks before you enter the river Rhône at Lyons, a distance of 151 miles. These locks are larger than those on the canals you have just left, and some are electrically operated.

At St.Jean-de-Losne – after three locks – the river is joined by the canal du Rhône au Rhin and after another two and a half miles by the Canal de Bourgogne, one of the alternative routes to the Med. from Paris. As a result of the confluence of these two canals the volume of barge traffic steadily increases.

The first large town on the Saône is Chalons-sur-Saône, reached after another five locks, and perhaps a good opportunity to stock up with tinned stuff in its supermarkets. The locks in the canals are a good source of fresh food like eggs and vegetables, even wine, at reasonable prices, because many of the lock-keepers seem to double the job of looking after the lock with that of market gardening.

The Canal du Centre joins the Saône at Chalons-sur-Saône, and again adds its barge traffic to the flow of craft on the river.

Despite the heavier barge traffic and its navigational obstacles the Saône is a lovely river. The hazards are not so drastic that you need to be on the immediate *qui vive*, rather they call for quick reaction when something happens, and a sharp look-out at all times so that you have as much time as possible in which to do something.

If you draw more than about five feet you may just ground on a sand bar without actually losing way. This happened to me when my wife was enthroned on the loo. The noise it made was frightening enough on deck but down below it sounded exactly as if we had run full tilt into a brick wall. No damage was done, except to our nerves of course.

You are still in wine country and Macon, Beaujolais and very many other famous names appear on the locks and in the places through which the canal runs.

A confusing factor on the Saône is the kilometre posts, which relate to all sorts of things except the distance from you to Lyons, and these marks are best ignored.

There is a strip map of the Saône, entitled *Le Saône de Lyon á Corre*, obtainable from *Editions Maritimes et d'Outre-Mer*, 17, Rue Jacob, Paris, (VI), and this is very useful to enable you to avoid the *cléonages* and make sure that you are keeping in the channel. Local opinion is that for boats drawing less than about two metres, providing you keep to the middle third of the river, you will have no problems, assuming that when the channel moves from the centre you do follow it.

After you leave Chalons-sur-Saône there are only four locks and a run of six miles and you are in Lyons, where you tie up at the Port de Plaisance. There is now only one more stretch of water to negotiate and you are in the Med. The dream grows nearer.

THE RHONE
The Rhône has a reputation as a dangerous river with torrents and waterfalls and weirs and rocks and sandbanks and rapids and floods: you name a fluvial hazard and it's on the Rhône. There are many people who have taken a yacht down the Rhône and have dined out on it ever since.

The Rhône has changed considerably over the last ten years. A vast civil engineering programme has resulted in the canalisation, or by-passing, of long stretches of river, and the construction of vast barrages, which are part of the French hydro-electric system. Modern locks of great depth and advanced design have been built.

Eventually, when the programme is completed, it will be possible for a 1000 ton barge to travel from the North Sea to the Med. through the canals.

Entering a big lock on the Rhône – L'Ecluse de Donzère

The effect of this tremendous expenditure of money and effort has been to transform the Rhône. To travel down it in a yacht is no longer the dangerous ordeal it once was. And as a result it is no longer obligatory to hire a pilot even though they still offer their services.

The commercial craft which work the river still employ them, however, because the Rhône has not been finally tamed.

One can buy a strip map at Lyons, and many people will say that a reasonably experienced yachtsman with the aid of the strip map and the exercise of plenty of caution should have no trouble running down the Rhône to the Med.

Here is a decision, then, which each owner must take for himself. To hire a pilot, which costs money, or to buy a strip map, which also costs money, though not anything like as much, and go solo?

My advice, not only based on experience but on the

experiences of others, is that it is still prudent to take a pilot, at least for the next year or so.

I have seen a 28 footer high and dry right in the middle of the river at a place where any right-minded person would have said was exactly where the main channel would run. In fact the channel ran along the bank, a hundred yards away, and it was quite impossible for any vessel drawing more than a couple of feet to get near enough to assist her. The owner was wading ashore in a wet suit, and the only way that I could see of getting his boat back into deep water was to hire a helicopter, one of the heavy-lift type, and use it as an airborne crane.

What had happened, I imagine, is that the level of water had dropped very suddenly — perhaps because flood water had dissipated itself and the river had dropped to its normal level and caught the skipper unawares.

The Rhône current still flows strongly in many places and

The famous Pont d'Avignon.

the channel can shift about as banks build up or scour away. Passing under some of the bridges, where the channel is constricted by the presence of the piers, can be risky unless you know the currents. The bridge at Avignon, *'sous le pont d'Avignon'* and not *'sur'*, is one bridge where there are heavy whirlpools and eddies, and it is said locally that if someone drowns at Avignon the body will not rise to the surface for several miles downstream.

The Rhône, like the Saône, has its *cléonages*, too, and it is still apt to sudden changes in its levels as a result of rain or drought or snow melting inland, so that these walls are not always visible.

So — take a pilot. The cost can be slightly reduced by two yachts proceeding in convoy, line astern, and sharing. Even so this can be a precarious business unless the second yacht follows exactly in the wake of the first.

The most famous of the pilots is M. Pariset, who has become something of a legend in his own lifetime. There are others equally competent, and you may also be able to do a deal with one of the company pilots who normally work full-time for a barge operator but who may not be averse to earning a few francs in his holiday by turning it into a busman's holiday. He won't undercut the other pilots, though.

The *Chef du Port de Plaisance* will put you in touch with someone reliable. Current cost is about £35, but like everything else, inflationary pressures operate, and prices rise constantly.

Lyons itself is a fascinating place. It is built at the confluence of the Saône and the Rhône, and has an atmosphere all its own, and a walk in the town after dark — for me at any rate — revived strong memories of the most sinister of French gangster films! Here it could all have happened!

The town also has a Roman amphitheatre in a very good state of preservation, and it is still used as a stage for TV spectaculars from time to time. If you want to declaim Shakespeare in a setting which is really appropriate to the plays he set in Roman times you could not find a better place.

Oddly enough the thespian theme is also carried on at the

Port de Plaisance where the gentleman who runs the place bears a remarkable resemblance to Marlon Brando playing Napoleon.

A day or so at Lyons is also worthwhile because it will give you an opportunity to rest your muscles after the unfair exertions of lock-bashing. You have worked your last lock, in all probability, for some little while, and lock-keepers elbow will soon become a thing of the past.

From Lyons to Arles, where the pilot normally disembarks, is 173 miles and at the time of writing there are seven locks. Thanks to the current this journey can be done comfortably in two days.

The gates lift up at this Rhône lock.

The locks themselves are probably the easiest you will ever go through, despite their size and the magnificence of the civil engineering. The design allows the water to drain away at a tremendous rate, yet there are no whirlpools or eddies, and the bollards float, so that they descend with you. There is thus no need to worry about slackening warps, and there is so little movement of water in the horizontal plane that there is really little need to tie up at all. The whole operation is as smooth as riding in a lift.

The most impressive lock is l'Ecluse de St.Pierre, near Bollene, where you drop 86ft in about six minutes. At the bottom of the lock the walls tower over you and an optical illusion (or just plain cowardice) made me feel that they were about to fall in on me.

Arles itself is another place of considerable interest. It boasts many Roman remains in good condition, and until the Middle Ages had great prosperity as a seaport. In those days the town was nearer the sea than it is now, and a much shorter canal than the extant Canal d'Arles à Bouc enabled large ships to bring their cargoes right into the city.

After you drop the pilot at Arles you have three options for the final short run into the Med. You can follow the Rhône down to the sea through its delta, a reckless course of action because of the banks and the tortuous channel which add up to almost certain trouble for the yachtsman who attempts it. You can continue down the river to Port St.Louis, a distance of about 26 miles, and which brings you to a lock which enables you to pass into the Golfe de Fos, which is the Mediterranean itself, and which is the route I would suggest. Or you can enter the Canal d'Arles à Port Bouc, which also discharges into the Golfe de Fos.

If you take the second choice you will find the run from

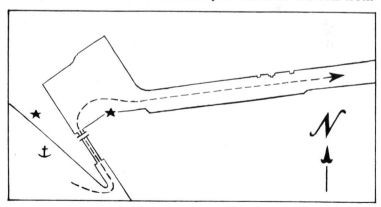

Port St Louis du Rhône. The anchor shows where you can tie up while you wait to lock through.

Arles presents no problems, and at Port St.Louis there is a wharf in the main stream of the river to which a number of derelict barges are tied up, slowly fading away like old soldiers, and to which you too can make fast until you are ready to lock through. You will probably want a full day, a day of good weather, ahead of you when you actually enter the Med.

The channel in the cut leading to the lock meanders a little, and the cut itself is blocked to some extent by moored local craft. Once through the lock a canalised stretch of water leads into the Golfe itself, and a marina lies on your starboard hand a short distance from the lock. The Med. itself is non-tidal this far east, so there is no hassle about having to lock through only at tide times.

The Canal d'Arles à Bouc is about thirty miles in length and boasts four locks. The level of water in it is uncertain due to the effects of the sea running into the canal from the east and the changes in the level of the Rhône when it floods or dries up. There may well be less than six ft. six ins. over the sill in the lock at Arles and perhaps only just over five feet in the canal. At the time of writing the canal is closed to enable

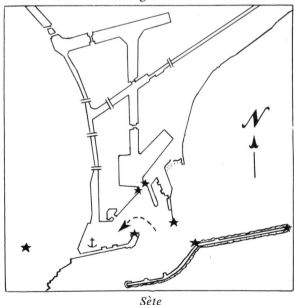

Sète

work to be done on it but there are hopes that it will be back in operation by spring 1974. The tunnel which connects the Etang de Beurre with Marseilles is closed and is unlikely to be re-opened.

There is yet another possibility, which is to enter the Canal du Rhône à Sète at Beaucaire, a few miles before Arles. This canal runs into Sète, 62 miles away, and a little over 50 miles to the West, through the Bassin de Thau, which is the back door to Sète, so to speak, and the canal is narrow, with passing places every mile or so.

The normal depth of the water is alleged to be six feet six inches. There are times when the canal is closed because the level of the water at either end can vary to a greater extent than the locks can cater for. This is due to winds raising the level in the Bassin de Thau at the western end or drying up at the eastern end, or to the Rhône flooding. In addition two rivers cut through the canal and there is no control over the volume of water. When they are in flood the canal is impassable.

Hence the only route which offers no problems is the one through the lock at Port St.Louis.

So having decided which of these routes you will take you will leave Arles, having recovered already, I hope, from the worst effects of lock-keepers elbow. You will by now have almost certainly experienced a *mistral.* More of these later: for the moment it is sufficient to observe that they are very cold winds which blow strongly down the Rhône Valley and can have the immediate effects of hastening your journey down stream, of making sweaters by day a necessity and a cabin heater equally so by night, and of gradually driving you out of your mind the longer they last.

The seas they create in the Golfe de Fos and the Golfe de Lyons are so treacherous that the lock-keeper at Port St. Louis may well bar you from passing through his lock if he believes that the weather is too bad.

Port St.Louis has a rather uninteresting and smelly little harbour which for some reason, invoked memories for me of Egypt: perhaps the dust and sand in the air and the smell of the place, partly compounded of sand and dust and partly of Mediterranean plumbing and sewage disposal.

Port de Bouc is a mass of oil refineries and tank farms tacked on to a pleasant little town with a good street market and an abominable smell emanating from the refineries. It is reminiscent of Port Victoria on the Medway or Canvey Island or Grangeworth, an affront to civilised people. However it is a good place to take on fuel.

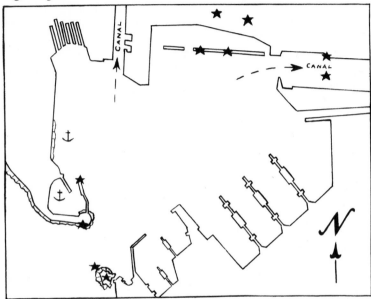

Port de Bouc

Arles is the place to raise your mast, because there are no more bridges below the town. While you rest from the labour of stepping it and setting up the rigging you will be able to make a pilgrimage to another bridge, the one which Vincent Van Gogh immortalised and which now bears his name. It is situated a short walk along the Canal d'Arles à Bouc.

A last general word on canals and locks before the magic moment when you pass through the one at Port St.Louis.

Some locks are seasonal in character, and are left open at both ends at certain times of year, others may not be in use for some other reason. Improvements are being made all the time to the whole system.

Down to the Med.

Hence the total number of locks you pass through may not
tally with the statistics, which means that sometimes you
may find yourself further along the canals than you
expected. So, there is a reason!

One question I have not attempted to answer in the
passages about the canals is — where does one tie at night?
There is no easy answer.

You must try to find a place where your presence will not
obstruct the commercial traffic or other yachts, and where
your warps will not stop people from walking or riding
mopeds along the towpaths.

In the busy waterways a favourite place is alongside a
barge which is not working cargo or scheduled to move early
in the morning. And they do make very early starts! The
barge skipper will usually make you welcome if there is no
obstacle to your using him as a quay, and will probably
suggest an alternative if there is some reason why you should
try elsewhere.

The barges usually congregate several deep in the recognised barge night-mooring parks, and it is a bad move to be
first vessel there. You will have to make way for them, so it
will probably be better to keep travelling for another hour or
so until they have started to roost for the night.

In the canals, especially the rural ones, you can usually
find a sheltered stretch of bank where you can tie up to trees.
Pick a wide place so that barges have plenty of room to pass
you, and a place where there is plenty of water so that you
won't be washed up and stranded when the passage of a laden
barge takes all the water with it.

This is where your scaffold boards and pickets come into
their own, and where you will want to moor up with springs
and breast ropes to reinforce the normal warps. The surge of
a laden barge has to be seen to be believed in a narrow canal,
and next time I go I shall moor up for the night with steel
hawsers.

And now let's get on with it and pass through that lock at
Port St.Louis!

4. The Heart of the Dream

Turn left or turn right?

Once you have passed through that lock at Port St.Louis you are faced with a major decision — which way to head.

Turning left is fine providing you don't go too far or for too long, because if you do you will find yourself in the fashionable and expensive Riviera where everything is based on the blithe assumption that all visitors are millionaires. St. Tropez — well, if you do want to see BB in the flesh you can always do so at the cinema. Cannes? It is said, without any truth at all, I am sure, that the harbour is so overcrowded that even blood relatives of the harbour master have to apply years in advance for a berth, just for one night, and the really with-it folk put their children's names down for a berth at birth.

Monte Carlo? Well, there are other casinos on the continent.

In fact most dreamers will elect to turn right and follow the Spanish coast, where living is relatively cheap, the sun always shines (or nearly always), and the natives are guaranteed to be friendly. You will also want to escape from the Golfe de Lyons, the happy hunting ground of the dreaded *Mistral*, the cold wind to which I have referred earlier.

What we did worked out pretty well. We turned left from

Port St.Louis, and made a fairly short leg to Cassis, a distance of about 40 miles and which took us about seven hours. For a first cruise in the Med. nothing could better it. The sea dances and sparkles, the colour matches the travel posters, the sun blazes down, and your first dolphin may well appear.

The coast line is rugged, well-wooded and interesting, and Cassis itself is a charming little town, with enough tourist activity to encourage you ashore if your budget will run to eating out, yet sufficiently undeveloped to be worth a run off the boat even if you can't afford to dip your hand in your pocket.

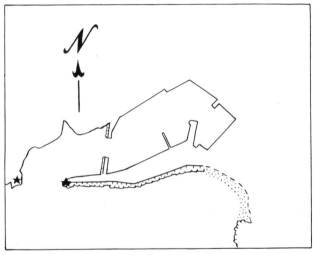

Cassis

Cassis will also give you an opportunity to moor *à la Méditerranée* for the first time, in reasonably sheltered conditions. More of this later, too, but what it is all about is dropping your anchor a few boat lengths from the quay while guiding your craft stern-first into a gap between what always appears to be the most expensive and most fragile yachts in the harbour.

Watching the inexperienced perform this evolution is an activity which often seems to be as popular for the natives as feeding Christians to the lions was for the Romans, and in both sports one often feels that the victims have about the same chances of winning.

From Cassis it is another day's sail to those delightful islands just east of Toulon; Porquerolles, Port Cros, and Levant, where the naturists have a colony, and you have to join them in the nude if you want to land.

It was anchoring in the sheltered bay at Port Cros which brought home to me just how marvellous yachting is in the Med. A casual glance over the bows when the anchor had just been dropped — and I could see through twenty feet of crystal clear water to the bottom. There was the anchor, nestling among the weeds, with a few small fish investigating this intruder in their world.

One couple of our acquaintance was so enamoured with de Cros that they spent the whole of their stay in the Mediterranean there. It is truly an idyllic place, perfect for re-charging the metaphysical batteries after the hard slog through the canals.

From here to Corsica is about 100 miles, but we turned west instead and retraced our footsteps to the Golfe de Lyons, and then cruised leisurely along the French and Spanish coasts to Gibraltar.

This is the plan we shall follow in this book, because it does seem the best way to get maximum benefit from your stay in the Med.

Let's turn left!

The first port of any size after you leave Port St.Louis is Marseilles. This is a centre for French yachting, and boasts sixteen clubs for sailing yachts and two more for motor craft. Moorings for yachts are in the Vieux Port, and the harbour has all the facilities of any major port. There is considerable commercial activity, with many deep-sea vessels of all types continually coming and going. Unless you particularly want to visit this historic old town to see whether or not its reputation is justified you might well prefer to miss it out.

Port St.Louis to Marseilles is about thirty miles, while Cassis is another ten. On your way along the coast you pass other harbours like La Ciotat, Bandol, Port St.Pierre on Isle d'Embiez, which is connected to the mainland by ferry, La Seyne-sur-Mer, a very busy fishing port, Toulon, a large and bustling naval base, Le Lavandou, and the new marina at

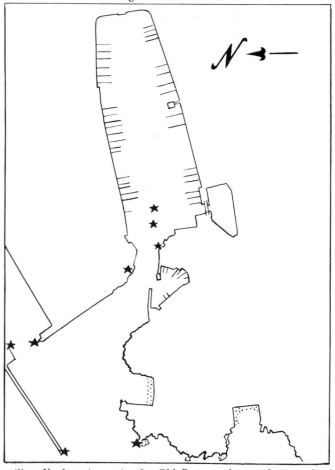

Marseilles. Yachts tie up in the Old Port at the northern end of the harbour.

Bormes-les-Mimosas. Much further east and you will be in the fashionable part of the Riviera.

The pearl in this oyster is Ile de Cros. There are two anchorages on the island, Port Cros and Port Man, on the west and on the north sides of the island respectively, and equally delightful. At Ile de Cros the combination of clear water and lush scenery is so exciting that it is easy to believe that you are in the South Seas.

At Port Cros there is a jetty to which you can tie up if you prefer this to anchoring, and there is deeper water at Port

Man, and a large mooring buoy for visitors. Inshore of the buoy there is about 25ft so that if you do anchor you won't have tons of chain to heave up afterwards.

You reach the shore from Port Man by rowing, and the channel is marked by inconspicuous buoys. Once ashore you can wander about the island for hours. The island is some kind of a nature reserve, and it is forbidden to develop it or even chop down a tree. It has a very small population, a few houses, a hotel, a restaurant, and a picturesque cemetery which is well worth a visit. The paths through the lush vegetation are marked and sign-posted, and provide some outstanding views over the water. You could say that I am well sold on Ile de Cros!

Before describing the run down the coasts of France and Spain towards Gibraltar it would be wise to devote a little time to a discussion of the weather in the Med. Although the Med. is truly what the Pilot describes as a favoured region, it

Aerial view of Marseilles.

can also be a treacherous place for a small-boat sailor who allows himself to be seduced by all those travel posters showing half naked dolly-birds lolloping in the sun into believing that there are no such things as gales.

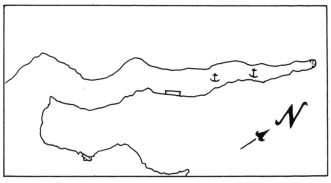

Port-Miou

DON'T UNDERESTIMATE THE WEATHER IN THE MED.

Gales there certainly are. St Paul was ship-wrecked on Malta by a *Gregale*, and a *Mistral* imperilled the life of the famous Roman Emporer Claudius in Gallicia Narbonnensis, as the Golfe de Lyons was then known. The designs of the modern Mediterranean in-shore fishing boats, with a great sheer and a highly flared bow, reflect the fact that they are not built for exclusively fine-weather work.

It is true that gales are most frequent in the winter, from November to April, but in the summer there are frequent shallow local depressions which produce strong winds up to gale strength in the limited areas they effect.

These gales have local names and local characteristics. I have mentioned the *Mistral* several times already. This is the prevailing unpleasant wind in the Rhône Valley and Golfe de Lyons. People in the north of France scoff at *Mistrals*, alleging that the fishermen of the south invoke them as an excuse to avoid working on hot days. This slur is quite unjustified.

A *Mistral* arrives suddenly and kicks up a big short steep sea very quickly. No prudent seaman gets caught out in one, least of all a fisherman, who stands to lose valuable gear.

It is said that a *Mistral* always lasts for a multiple of three days — 3, 6, 9, 12, 15 even. It is a steady cold wind that sweeps down the Rhône Valley bringing with it the icy breath of the Alps. It flays the nerves after a while, and it is said that a succession of *Mistrals* drove the painter Van Gogh out of his mind — and I have no difficulty in accepting that this is true.

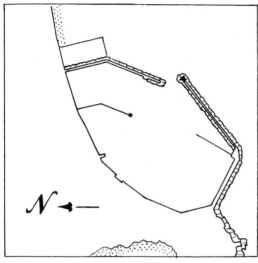

Bandol

Mistrals are caused by cold air being sucked into the north west Mediterranean from the north and north west on the flank of a depression in the Golfe de Lyons or the Gulf of Genoa. They funnel down the Rhône Valley which increases their strength. A branch of this air stream flows across Catalonia, where it is known as the *Tramontana*, and another branch is drawn down the valley of the Ebro, where it is called the *Mestral*.

These winds effect the Balearics, where a *Tramontana* plus a *Mistral* can add up to a considerable blow, and one hears frightening stories of the havoc such conditions can cause in the marina at Palma in the winter.

The strength of these winds increases with the distance away from the coast and their direction is influenced by the direction in which the coast runs. For example, near Cabo de Oropesa the *Tramontana* swings westerly.

In the shelter of a headland or a land-locked harbour one

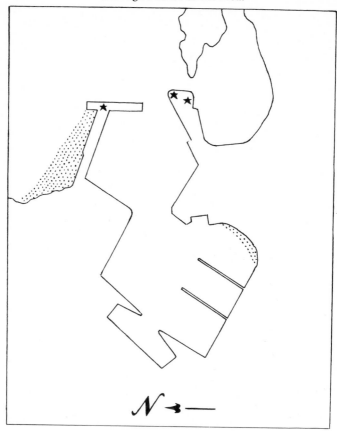

Port St. Pierre on the Ile d'Embiez

can be deceived very easily about the strength of a *Mistral*. The heat of the sun, if you are out of the wind, and the subtly insidious effect of the propaganda from the travel firms can influence your judgement if you are not careful. This is when one should seek the advice of a fisherman or a harbour official. It doesn't matter if your mastery of the language is slight.

'Tramontana, Senor?'

'Si, Senor, Tramontana!'

The strength of the wind can be gauged by the intensity of your informant's reply, by the urgency of his desire to warn you. A really nasty blow will lead to gesticulations, eye-rolling, drawings in the dust, and a walk arm-in-arm to the harbour wall.

In eastern Spain an unusually clear atmosphere is warning of the likelihood of a *Mestral*.

In the Straits of Gibraltar you can expect mostly easterlies or westerlies. In the spring and in the autumn you often get easterlies along the coasts and at the same time westerlies in the middle of the Straits, and as the depressions move in through the Straits strong south westerly winds can spring up, known locally as *Vendevales*. These winds decrease in strength as they approach the southern coast of Spain, and they may veer to the west or the north west.

In the summer, banks of cumulo-nimbus from the north-east, often obscuring the horizon and preceded by a heavy swell, indicate the arrival of the famous Gibraltar *Levanter*. This is a strong easterly wind, and the clouds which build up over the Rock itself are reminiscent of the 'table-cloth' which forms over Table Mountain at Cape Town. These clouds disperse as the wind strengthens.

A friend of mine called Kevin found himself wind-bound for weeks in Tangier by a *Levanter*. This could have had serious consequences, because one has to be a little strong-minded at the best of times in Tangier if one wishes to avoid becoming involved in any of the sordid illegal activities which seem to flourish there so openly, and as one's money runs out so temptation clearly becomes even harder to fight. The solution is to do as we did and leave the harbour at about

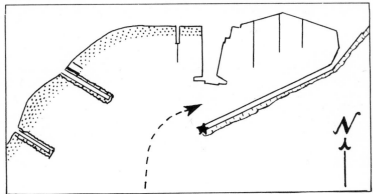

Le Lavandou

four in the morning, before the wind has had time to build up.

Associated with the *Levanter* is the *Levante* and the *Llevantade*, which originate in the north east and occur near the Spanish coast. The *Levante* is often an offspring of the *Levanter*, and is frequently preceded by the arrival of a heavy swell, as much as 24 hours in advance of the wind.

On the west coast of Sardinia they experience a strong wind from the west to south west, known as the *Libeccio*. This is associated with the *Vendevales* we talked about earlier.

Don't think from all this that you never get souther-lies in the western Med. They are experienced when a depression moving east is near enough to the North African coast to draw air from the desert. This wind is called a *Scirocco*, and it can be so hot as a result of the desert air that it will

A corner of the new marina at Bormes. Many of the yachts here are for charter.

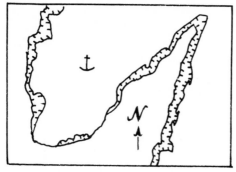

Port Man

wither vegetation. It soon picks up moisture in its passage over the sea, which results in a lower temperature but high humidity, which can be very uncomfortable.

I recall several years ago, when I was one of the crew of the Union-Castle Liner, Dunottar Castle, and we were on passage through the Med, that the ship became coated with fine brown dust. This was sand from the desert, carried over maybe 200 miles of sea by a *Scirocco*. When it rains in these conditions you get the phenomenon known as 'red rain'. It amounts almost to raining mud! In North Africa this wind is also known as a *Chihli* or a *Chibli* and in Spain as a *Leveche*.

I have already mentioned the *Gregale*. This is a strong north-easterly wind caused by high pressure in the Balkans and low pressure in the Gulf of Sidra and in the southern Ionian Sea. It blows mainly in the winter and at times reaches gale force.

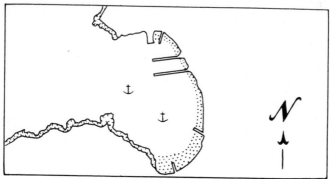

Port Cros

There are obvious dangers in making a passage when a *Mistral* or *Levanter* is expected. The sudden arrival of quick steep seas, squalls, gale force winds, and the possibility of a change in wind direction, which could in some circumstances put you on to a lee shore, these are not conditions to be lightly experienced.

In addition, and peculiar to the Med., is the effect that these strong winds can have on the direction and strength of the currents. Normally, currents tend to flow anti-clockwise round the basin bounded by North Africa, Sicily, Southern France and Southern Spain. But a *Levanter*, say, can deflect this circulatory system, and induce strong on-shore sets where normally there are none.

Further, these strong winds can produce water spouts, especially near Gibraltar, Cabo de Gata and near the Balearics. I have never seen a water spout in the Med. myself, and having been near a couple in the English Channel I am not sorry.

Sète harbour (picture: Hugh Mcknight)

It is not always easy for an English yachtsman to obtain, let alone understand, a weather forecast in Mediterranean waters. How then, can you avoid ever getting caught out in one of these unpleasant winds? Asking a fisherman or a harbour master is good policy whatever the weather looks like. And following their advice is better.

If in doubt stay in harbour. Don't let that travel poster spiel fool you. Out there — it can BLOW! If you do get caught out make for shelter as fast as you can, and watch your navigation all the way. A *Mistral* can be as nasty as an English Channel gale.

This is not intended to put you off the Dream. It is meant as a plea for you to be as aware of the weather in the Med. as you would in home waters, and to be conscious all the time of the likely direction of gales.

A lot of the time the travel posters are dead right, but not always. Now repeat after me:-

'*Mistral aujourd'hui, Monsieur?*'

TO RETURN TO OUR MUTTONS

So this is why I advocate getting across the Golfe de Lyons as soon as possible. The further south of the Franco-Spanish border you are the less chance of gales.

I have already suggested some of the ports you are likely to want to use in this area. On the way west and south you will no doubt try to visit places you haven't been into before even though you are retracing your steps.

One place in which you will almost certainly want to stop over is Sète, the exit port into the Canal du Rhône a Sète and one of the possible ways into the Canal du Midi. It is a bustling, busy little town, where you will almost certainly find tied up at least one well-known yacht, either in the marina or in the canal, and it is the venue for the jousting tournaments which are held between rowed skiffs late in the summer. Sète, too, is a place where you can use your Shell credit card to refuel.

The whole of the area between the Rhône delta and the Spanish border is being developed in a tremendously ambitious scheme which is known as the *Languedoc-Roussillon* development. For ten years now a determined

Port Bacarat; part of the Languedoc-Roussillon development. Typical new Mediterranean marina.

anti-mosquito campaign has been waged to rid the whole of the area of these malignant pests, with almost complete success, while civil engineering works on an enormous scale have been started. The plans when they are turned into fact, will have created a vast marina plus housing complex all along the coast, with eventually over 10,000 marina yacht berths, each with its own electricity and water point, each marina located about fifteen miles from the next, and with hotels, flats and villas providing accommodation for many thousands of people.

At Gruissan, for example, there will be a 1500 boat marina, and the scheme provides for housing for 50,000 people, in an area encompassing Saint Pierre-sur-Mer, Narbonne-Plage, Gruissan itself of course, and Gruissan-Plage. At Leucate-Barcares there are already 1500 moorings available out of a planned 2000, and 12½ miles of canals and harbours will be excavated.

At the moment the mooring fees are reasonable for marina

berths. The first day for a visitor is free and thereafter a 26 footer pays about 60p a day or £3 a week, £9 a month or £60 per annum. So long as you keep on the move — or else stay for a year it is cheap to use these marinas.

Whether of not these schemes are included in the material of which dreams are made is debatable. But there are still plenty of unspoilt fishing villages along the Spanish coast which have berths for visiting yachts, and I cannot but feel that readers of this book, the real Dreamers, will not be happy for long in the raw concrete wildernesses of Languedoc-Roussillon. The situation is akin to the Maplin area of Essex: now is the time to visit and savour before it all disappears for ever.

At the time of writing the best place to call in after Sète is Agde if you wish to avoid the new developments. Agde lies up the river Hérault, and is a delightful town with a character all its own. The river is normally placid, but heavy rain turns it into a tomato-coloured torrent as a result of the silt brought down from inland.

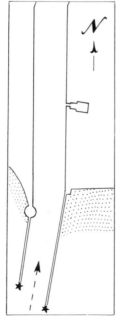

The entrance to the river Herault.

You can tie up along the river bank short of the town or try for a berth within the confines of Agde itself.

There is more water in the entrance than is quoted in some text books; not six feet but a great deal more.

If you do call in here it would be well worth taking the opportunity to make a quick reconnaissance of the beginning of the Canal du Midi and the famous Round Lock which marks the canal proper. Almost immediately after the stone bridge which carries main road traffic from one bank of the Hêrault to the other there is a 'cut' on the left which is spanned by a Bailey bridge of war-time vintage – or it was at the time of writing. This is the entrance to the canal. It is only a short walk to the Round Lock.

The 'cut' is at a very acute angle to the river, and it is said that if you can get round this corner and under the Bailey bridge you will be able to pass the whole of the route to the Garonne without any problems.

So the moral is that if you intend to take this route home and you are dubious about being able to clear the bridges, take a tape measure and a lead line and measure the Bailey bridge. I did this at what I thought was an early hour of the day, when no one would be about to ask what the devil I thought I was up to. The French are early risers, however, in Agde anyway, and I had a very quizzical crowd watching me by the time I had finished. And my French is quite inadequate for explaining away this kind of activity.

After Agde a recommended port of call is Port Vendres. This could well be the last French harbour you see for quite a while, so savour it while you may.

Port Vendres is a bustling lively little town with a quayside cafe society which is switched on, and is also very irritating if you have tied up on the quay below the cafe. Sleep is quite impossible until the last two-stroke mini-moped has roared its nerve-racking way into the night, unless you have been wiser than we were and found a berth in the marina. The harbour is well sheltered, and is a good place in which to hide if the *Mistral* is blowing.

And then over the border into Spain. Don't forget to swap courtesy flags on the way!

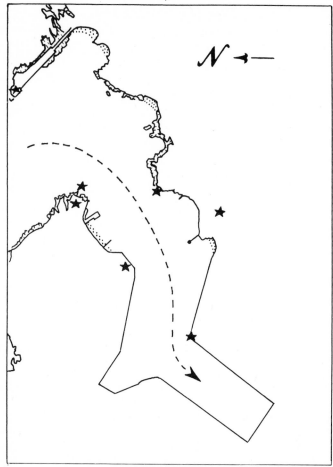

Port Vendres

NAVIGATION IN THE MED.

Before describing the trip down the Spanish coast it might be a good idea to discuss the differences between navigation in the Med. and that of home waters.

It is simpler in the Med., of course, because once east of Malaga there are no tides to worry about. The rise and fall at Gib. is only a few feet, and the range rapidly diminishes as you go east, until by Malaga it is nominal, though still noticable.

In fact I nearly broke my neck in Malaga because of the

111

tides. A slimey step leading down into the water was just covered at high water and just uncovered at low water, and leaping on to it from *Rolling Wave* I put my whole weight on to a sheet of what might well have been ice. The result was one airborne yachtsman landing with a crash which nearly broke several vertebrae.

This lack of tides has the beneficial result that all harbours and anchorages are always accessible, and one is thus free of the traditional UK tyranny of having to 'work the tides', with all this implies.

You don't have to get up at three in the morning just to catch the tide: you can lie in until a more civilised hour like 4 am. If you arrive at your destination an hour later than planned it doesn't mean that you have to wait for hours until the flood enables you to enter. Nor do you have to be up half the night tending warps when you aren't sure of the patterns of tidal behaviour in a strange harbour.

Is it neaps of springs? If you are as dim as I am it is a major relief to escape the involved calculations which you are faced with in the Channel ports, for example, and which you will be faced with again before you get home.

Even better, you avoid the other major frustration often experienced in tidal waters — making two knots forward under sail in a light breeze while a three knot tide pushes you backwards.

There are currents to contend with in the Med., however. The *Mediterranean Pilot, Volume I,* tells you all about them. It points out that only about one-third of the amount of water which evaporates is replaced by the rivers which flow into the Med. If you have seen the Rhône in flood you may share my incredulity, and you may also ask why it is that the Med. doesn't eventually dry up completely. The mean sea level in the central Med. may drop by as much as one and a half feet below normal, in March and April.

Surface water is flowing through the Straits of Gibraltar all the time to compensate for the overall loss, and a current is thus created. It follows the north coast of Africa as far as Egypt, gradually weakening as it goes, swings north up the shores of Palestine and then turns west round the back of Cyprus and into the Aegean. West of Crete some funny things start to happen, depending on the time of year, but speaking generally a fairly weak current follows the west coast of Italy in a northerly direction and then runs west along the Riviera and continues to follow the Spanish coast right back to Gibraltar.

If you split the Med. into two basins on either side of Malta, the current systems are an anti-clockwise movement of water in each basin, just like two enormous bath tubs.

These basic surface currents are not very strong and are therefore disrupted all the time by winds and by local temporary drift currents, and thus, as the *Pilot* says, it is possible to find, in any part of the Med., a current setting towards any point of the compass.

Where does this leave you? In my view, when making a passage, estimating the influence which observed local conditions may have upon the basic circulatory system. In other words, when planning cruises and plotting courses, to some extent making inspired guesses!

This is not good enough, of course. It means that a lot of attention has to be paid to estimating actual leeway, and this in turn means getting accurate fixes all the time and plotting them on the chart so that your actual leeway can be calculated and allowed for.

Although the basic currents are weak, around ½ to ¾ knots, sets of up to five knots are not unknown and two to three knots is fairly common.

If leeway is not observed when these sets are operating, a yacht sailing in light airs – and in the Med. when it's not blowing too hard, the airs normally are light! – may well find herself in some other place than the one in which she intended to be.

If you are coast-hopping it is thus possible that you may make port in the dark and not in daylight, and if the harbour is strange to you, which probably will be the case, you will then curse yourself for having to sort out a strange place for the first time in the dark.

As in tidal waters, an early appreciation of unexpected sets enables the appropriate corrective action to be taken, and in the Med. this usually means rigging the iron topsail.

A characteristic of the western Med. is the lack of buoys.

One feels that the French have exhausted all their stocks in Brittany and have had no buoy money in the kitty for years. The Spanish do not seem to be keen on buoys, period, but compensate for this by excelling at lighthouses. In daylight these are often the most easily identifiable features on their coasts. They light their harbours well, too. The Moroccans are good at both buoys and lighthouses.

The sketches in the *Pilot* are often so out of date as to be useless when it comes to trying to sort out which stretch of coast is which. For example, the drawing of Cabo de Tossa lighthouse is dated prior 1952, and it ignores all the hotels built over the last few years and which radically alter the whole aspect of the coast. Some of the sketches are dated 1880!

This is not as despair-making as one would expect, however. The fact that visibility is usually pretty good in the Med. helps, though fog and mist are prevalent in the Straits of Gibraltar.

You can usually pick up your landfall from a greater distance than you would in home waters. Until you become used to this your estimating of distances will tend to be rather inaccurate.

At night it is easy to think that a lighthouse which is actually ten miles off is a buoy only one mile away, because there may be no 'loom'. This was my experience when making a landfall at Tossa at night after a passage from Mallorca.

Lights on other craft can often be seen for greater distances than you are accustomed to, with the result that you will probably alter course if necessary long before you really need to.

Navigational aids on board? I don't think that an echo sounder is of great value in the Med., except when you want to check a depth to calculate how much cable to let out. There are very few shoals and deep water usually continues very close inshore. They say that you can always tell an English yacht in the Med. because the ingrained habits learned at home of always giving a wide berth to every shore, results in the Englishman being about three miles out to sea when the locals are buzzing along twenty yards away from the rocks. The rocks usually drop straight down into a lot of fathoms, so you are quite safe close in.

Very useful is a D/F set. Our Seafix certainly earned its keep when we were in the Med., both as a hand bearing compass and as a D/F set for getting radio bearings on beacons.

There are nearly sixty marine and aeronautical beacons between Gib. and Palermo. I got some pretty good cocked hats at times with that lot, thin ones, fat ones, even pin-points sometimes. And if you do get lost, even close inshore, you can always locate yourself with a D/F.

Other essential aids to navigation include *Reeds Almanac,* a full set of Admiralty charts, although these are nothing like as up to date or accurate as those applying to home waters and the *Mediterranean Pilot Voume I.* The *West Coast of Spain and Portugal Pilot* is useful if you intend to cross over to Tangier. A barometer is always vital and so is a radio for getting weather forecasts if you can understand the language! The ability to recognise key words like *Mistral* and *Tramontana* will help considerably.

What you are most unlikely to need is things like sextants, logs, speedos and so on, certainly not radar, unless you intend making long passages, in which case you will already have the appropriate equipment.

The Golfe de Lyons with its sudden gales and the Straits of Gibraltar with its currents, tidal rips and fogs are the only two parts of the Western Med. where navigation is anything but a doddle – providing you remember about those currents!

ONCE AGAIN BACK TO OUR MUTTONS!
Spain is rich in harbours suitable for small yachts to use, right down the Mediterranean coast.

First one over the border is Port Bou, about eight miles from Port Vendres, with nothing much to recommend it, and after about the same distance lies the natural harbour of Puerto Selva, picturesque and attractive but with little in the way of facilities. After another eight miles again are the twin havens of Port Lligat and Cadaques, on either side of a rocky promontory. Cadaques is a recognised harbour, has an attrac-

Port Lligat

tive small town with a street market where fruit and fish can be obtained cheaply, and a bodega where wine and sherry can be bought in large glass containers at incredibly low prices. The anchorage is fairly close in to the waterfront and there are a few patches of rocks to watch out for as you enter.

But on the northern side of the promontory is Lligat, which is one of my favourite places. This is a natural harbour, well sheltered, with only one hotel and Salvador Dali's private residence, which looks something like a cross between a basket of overgrown white onions and a Mexican hacienda, very attractive too, visible from the sea. There is a church and one or two other small buildings around to form the village, plus a caravan site, the occupants of which never seem to stray to the beach.

Don't attempt to anchor too close in to the beach in this case, because it shelves and gets very shallow quite a long way out.

If you want anything you just row ashore and walk over the headland into Cadaques.

116

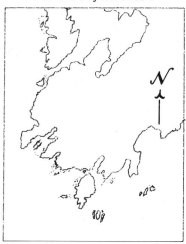

Cadaques

There is only room in Port Lligat for a handful of yachts, but the chances are that you will have it to yourself. This is one of the reasons why I favour it. There is a touch of the 'Bali-Hi's' about Port Lligat.

Round the headland from Cadaques lies the tourist resort of Rosas, which also has a harbour. This lies some distance from the bright lights and gay noises of the hotel scene, however, and boasts a fishing industry large enough to support a fish market and auction.

The next port down the coast is Estartit, another fishing village which has developed into a holiday resort, but without the tasteless hotel development which has ruined so many of them. This is followed by Palamos, a larger place altogether, with a harbour used by larger commercial freighters as well as the traditional fishing fleet. It is a place to call in for repairs, and supports a marina and a modern *Club Nautico,* which lies at the inshore end of the long breakwater on the starboard hand as you enter.

Another well-sheltered harbour is the next one down the coast, San Felieu de Guixols, said to be the largest town on the Costa Brava, certainly one of the more sophisticated. Here again there is usually a berth available for the visitor at the *Club Nautico.* If you want to visit the barbarism of the bull fight you should be able to do so at San Felieu.

117

Ampuriabrava, in the Bay of Rosas, where a marina complex is under completion.

An alternative harbour, fifteen miles further down the coast, is Blanes, which supports a large fishing fleet, whose members seem to respect the yacht moorings as being reserved for yachts. The same distance down the coast is Arenys de Mar, which boasts a large marina style mooring complex and an expensive yacht club. On the way you pass Tossa del Mar which has a recognised anchorage for yachts and which many find charming.

The harbour at Arenys is segregated from the town by a railway and a road with an underpass to enable you to reach

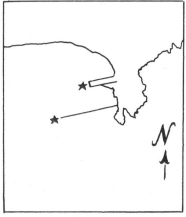

Palamos

the one from the other. The town itself seems to have been largely ignored by the people who spoil places with neon and chrome, and I personally find it a most interesting place, though its attraction may be lessened if you stay too long because here the marina makes a charge. You may be able to find a berth on the wall opposite the marina, by the fishing boats, but there are underwater rocks to watch out for as you come alongside.

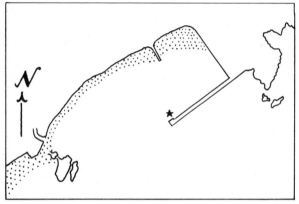

Blanes Bay

Badalona, some eighteen miles further along the coast, is a highly industrialised place with no appeal to Dreamers at all, and it is far better to sail on for another five miles to Barcelona.

Barcelona makes its presence felt from afar. Not only is it a large town, heavily populated, with a very busy commercial dock area, and a long mole enclosing the harbour, with the result that its industrial atmosphere, chimneys and so on, leave you in no doubt that you are a few miles away from the haunt of modern industrial man, but also the water changes colour as you approach the harbour. Some of the effluent of modern industrial man finds its way into the sea!

There is a large marina in Barcelona, which you reach by steaming right through the middle of the harbour, passing three separate cross quays on your port hand and turning to port round the last one. The marina then lies ahead of you.

Notices on the ends of the pontoons, in different languages, indicate where the visitor can berth, depending on the

119

size of the boat. This is an idea which should be copied elsewhere. A long stay in Barcelona can be expensive, unless you can make an arrangement with the harbour master to tie up alongside a harbour wall.

The *Club Nautico* here has a good reputation for being helpful to visitors, and they certainly get plenty of practice.

You will want to visit the town here. The best way is by walking or even by taxi, which will be relatively cheap. We took a taxi while we were in Barcelona, piloted by a very friendly and helpful taxi driver, who frightened the life out of us by driving with one hand and no forward look-out activity at all while he thumbed through a 1890 guide book to the town in English so that we could read all about the sights as we erratically drove past them.

There is a life-size replica of Christopher Columbus' Santa Maria in the harbour, and aerial gondolas traverse the city on high wires rather like horizontal cable railways. There are museums by the dozen, or so it seems, shops, restaurants, *poste restante* can be organised here, repairs undertaken; it's all here in Barcelona.

It was in Barcelona that I was delighted to find a main dealer for Kelvins, with a comprehensive stock of spares and a wall decorated with photographs of the Queen on a horse. This was a relic of the years the 'guvnor' spent in Glasgow doing his time in Kelvin's factory, where his son was currently following in dad's footsteps.

Barcelona is a good place to stock up with fuel and water, though water is charged for on the 'big-ship' basis at so many pesetas per ton, which makes it rather expensive for the yachtsman with something smaller under his feet than a cargo ship.

After leaving Barcelona the first harbour worth commenting on is Villaneuva Y Geltru. Scoot past De Garraf and Vallcarca as fast as you can. Villanueva is only about fifteen miles from Barcelona and boasts an inner as well as an outer harbour. Yachts moor near the yacht club or stern-to at a pontoon when there is room.

You will probably decide to carry on down the coast to Tarragona, where again there is a yacht club and also a public jetty where mooring is cheap. Tarragona is a good place to go

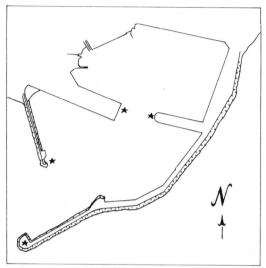

Tarragona

to for repairs, especially if slipping is required. It was in
Tarragona that I swam in the harbour, reluctantly because it
stank so much of fish, but of necessity to cool down after
working on the engine through the heat of the afternoon.
When I dried off in the sun my wife spent the first five
minutes picking bits of the corpses of fish from my beard.

An alternative to Tarragona is Cambrils, thirteen miles
down the coast. There are berths here for 200 yachts at the
yacht club and again the fishing fleet is kept away from the
yachts. The yacht club is said to be hospitable.

The next harbour down the coast is Ametlla de Mar, little
used by yachts, and the last harbour before the Ebro delta.
Cape Tortosa marks the extremity of the delta, an area of
shoaling sand banks which are created by the silt which the
river deposits outside its mouth. The sea is discoloured for
some distance from the river and the usual assorted river-
borne flotsam like trees, branches and bottles creates the
usual minor hazard for light construction yachts. It is a good
plan to give a reasonable berth to Cape Tortosa. If a north-
easter is blowing, however, the long fetch from Italy can kick
up a heavy sea, and you may do better to shelter inside the
cape.

The fishing boat which tied up to our anchor chain.
We both tried to negotiate for a few fish — and
finished up with a bucket full.

There is an anchorage at Puerto del Fangar, tucked away in the bay which is created partly by the delta of the Ebro and partly by the mainland. This is a delightful quiet secluded anchorage where it is highly unlikely that any other yacht will join you and where the noble sport of swimming starkers can be indulged in with no risk of the Guardia participating.

You need to feel your way in with some care as the water shoals fairly rapidly, another product of the silt of the Ebro.

When we were anchored here one morning, my wife Diana frolicking happily in the water in the nude, a small local fishing boat puttered round our stern and made fast to our anchor chain! As she came along our port side Diana discreetly swam along the starboard side, and eventually scrambled rapidly over the stern and into the shelter of a towel. A long frustrating dialogue then took place between us and the fishermen, and not for the first time I wished that I

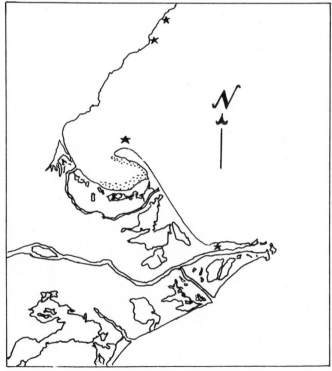

The Ebro Delta

could speak Spanish, particularly when a suggestion by us that we be allowed to buy a few of the fish they were removing from their nets — it was to do this that they had tied up to us — resulted in our receiving a whole bucket full of assorted catch. It proved quite impossible to get them to understand that we only wanted enough for our breakfast, so we lived on fish for the next four days!

It is unlikely that you will want to poke about up the river Ebro itself. On the south side of the delta is another anchorage, at Puerto de los Alfaques, not to be recommended when there is any Northing in the wind. There is also a small harbour called San Carlos de la Rapita, used by fishing boats mainly, though there is a yacht club with berths for visiting yachts.

Another fifteen miles to the south lies the harbour of Vinaroz which is largely monopolised by fishing boats, although there are limited facilities for yachts and also shops and a market.

Benicarlo, four-and-a-half miles away, is a small fishing harbour with water and fuel available and a few shops.

A better bet is Peniscola, about five miles further on, which lies behind a very conspicuous headland which is

The harbour at Benicarlo

crowned by a mediaeval castle. The history of the place goes back to Roman times. The castle is well worth a visit if you have the stamina to take you up the steep road to it.

Thirty-six miles further on is Castellon, another possible place in which to stop. The fishing boats have their own harbour to the left as you enter, the larger commercial ships tie up on the right, and the yacht club lies ahead with mooring trots just off the quay. Castellon is developing as an oil port and there are rigs off the coast nearby.

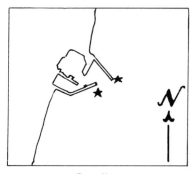

Castellon

The town is about two miles inland, a bus ride or a walk along a road running between orange groves. There are also a few shops at El Grao, just outside the harbour.

Fifteen miles further on is the harbour of Burriana, notable for its ship-breaker's yard and its fishing fleet. Like Castellon the walk takes you through the orange groves.

Another sixteen miles down the coast is Sagunto, a highly industrialised harbour which will not appeal to the Dreamer. But Valencia is only sixteen miles further on, the third largest harbour in Spain and a beautiful and interesting city. There is a yacht club here where you should be able to find a berth.

There is a tremendous amount to see in Valencia, including splendid museums. The best way to get to the centre of the town is to take a tram. From July 20 to 31 the annual July Fair is held, which ends with the famous battle of the flowers.

When we were there we tied up at a buoy, being over-awed by the splendour of the yacht club, and were invaded by

The Club Nautico at Castellon

millions of fruit flies overnight. Presumably these came from
one of the fruit ships which use the harbour.

Cullera, some seventeen miles away is the next harbour, a
short distance up the river Jucar, and entered between two
moles. With no local knowledge it may be best to miss out
Cullera in view of the un-marked shoals, and keep on for
Gandia, seventeen miles further on. This is not the most
beautiful of harbours, but you should be able to find a safe
and sheltered mooring here, probably at the yacht club which
lies on your starboard hand as you enter. At Gandia we saw a
ship with the unfortunate name of 'Manure'.

Fifteen miles away lies Denia a little to the north of the
conspicuous Cape Nao. Denia boasts two breakwaters with
the entrance in the middle. Here, too, the fishing fleet is
isolated in its own part of the harbour. The yacht club lies
ahead of you as you enter, with pontoon moorings in front
of it. It is a pleasant little town with good shopping facilities.

Another six miles away is Javea, a delightful little harbour
which poses the same problems as many others of having

The great freshwater lake at La Albufera, some miles inland from Valencia.

underwater obstructions along the quays. It is a popular harbour for cruising yachts, possesses good shops, and is a good place in which to hide.

Once past the massive Cape Nao you come to Calpe, fifteen miles from Javea. Calpe is primarily a fishing harbour and has good repair facilities. It lies in the shelter of a massive rock which looks rather like the more famous Rock of

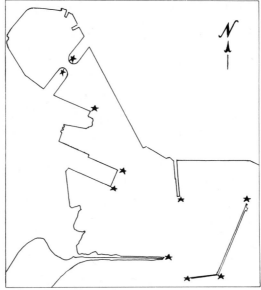

Valencia

Gibraltar from a distance, except that Gib. is many times larger than Penon de Ifach, as it is known.

The harbour at Calpe is still new, and was not even marked on the Admiralty chart when we were there. So we anchored in the bay outside what looked like a long wall, not realising that it was a harbour wall, and when the harbour officials came out in a small boat to ask what was wrong with their smashing new harbour we were too ashamed to admit

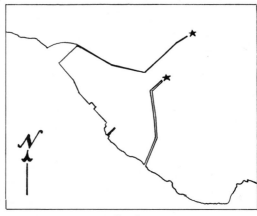

Denia

128

The very conspicuous headland, Penon de Ifach, with the new harbour of Calpe.

ignorance and pleaded that we preferred to anchor! The harbour walls are extended a little way under water and again provide a hazard to a deep draught yacht.

Calpe is a good place in which to buy fish, fresh and only just landed, and fairly cheap.

Four-and-a-half miles away is Altea, where you anchor in the middle of the harbour, well protected by two sea walls. It is a pleasant little place with shops and a market, but the inexorable tourist invasion is gradually robbing the place of its character. An alternative is Alicante, twenty-three miles further to the south.

The entrance to Alicante is dominated to starboard by a large Moorish castle, the castle of Santa Barbara. Coming from the north you have to follow the outer mole until you can turn hard to starboard round the small light-house, and then follow the wall back again on a reciprocal course, through the large commercial outer harbour, and then turn to port between the second pair of Light Towers and into the inner harbour.

Alicante. Yachts tie up stern-to on the wall running from the very tall buildings in the centre of the picture. Usually this wall is crammed tight with yachts.

Yachts tie up stern-to at the eastern wall. The moorings are often pretty crowded, but space can usually be found – or made – by the nautical equivalent of barging with the shoulders, in London commutor style.

Alicante is one of my favourite places. The harbour handles a variety of interesting cargoes, is very busy, and yet the yacht quay is far enough away from the commerce to have almost the atmosphere of a little village in its own right.

The town itself is attractive and lively. There are mosaic pavements, palm trees line many of the streets, and there are pleasant public squares with gorgeous public gardens. A favourite walk towards the end of the day is along the mosaic road which follows the harbour wall, where what seems like half the population of Alicante takes its evening stroll.

There are good sandy beaches, well patronized, and sightseeing is a rewarding activity.

The Moorish castle is well worth a visit. You reach this by taking a lift which runs in a shaft driven through the rock, entered by a tunnel the decor of which is reminiscent of Piccadilly Circus underground station.

Alicante is one of the places where I would recommend

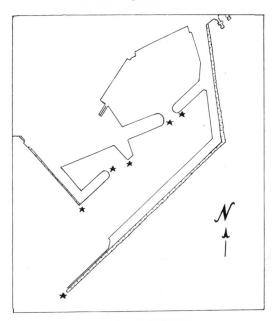

Alicante harbour

that you stop off for a couple of days and turn yourself into a tourist using the boat as an hotel, and taking a breather from voyaging. Spend a day on boat maintenance before you set off again. The further south you go the hotter the weather and the less likely you are to want to work on the boat, least of all in the engine compartment.

So perhaps the place to get things up to scratch is Alicante. There are good facilities here, and an expatriate Englishman named Bertie Mitchell who has fluent Spanish and a string of contacts a mile long who operates in the harbour area as a sort of Mr. Fix-it. Bertie is most helpful in solving any problem connected with boat, engine or gear, at a modest fee.

Nine miles south of Alicante is Sante Pola, a small fishing harbour where you can find a berth past the fishing boats on your starboard side after you have rounded the harbour wall, or alternatively you can anchor within the harbour wherever you can find room.

About seventeen miles further on is Torrevieja, where you

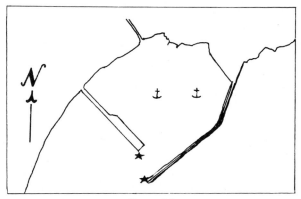

Torrevieja

will find a large harbour with a small marina within its boundaries, clearly visible when you enter between the harbour walls. Be prepared to moor stern-to here, an activity to which you may have become unaccustomed recently.

Some forty miles further on stands the commercial harbour of Portman, a place to be avoided unless heavy weather or trouble makes it advisable to find a harbour quickly. The same is true of Escombrera, six miles further on.

It is probably better to bash on and make for Cartegena, which is only a six mile passage. The harbour here is within an almost completely landlocked bay and is guarded by the ruins of castles. Yachts tie up by the club. Cartegena is a Spanish naval base, has a busy commercial harbour as well, boasts an arsenal and shipyards, plus a town of some size with good shopping facilities.

On your way down this particular stretch of coast you may well decide that the Dream is better realised by anchoring in a secluded and sheltered bay instead of seeking shelter in what may turn out to be an ugly, smelly and noisy commercial port. To be recommended are Punta de Estacio, a few miles after Torrevieja, and to a lesser extent, the anchorage off Carboneras. This is a fascinating little village with no harbour. To go ashore here you therefore have to row – or swim, which is not so crazy as it sounds. There is also a good restaurant in the village. The whole area is used for the production of cowboy films, made on location in the nearby deserts. We went mad at Carboneras and had a meal ashore,

132

and for the first — and last — time in our lives ate swordfish, a very tasty dish indeed.

Before continuing to describe the other harbours on the run down to Gibraltar it might be a good idea to pause and discuss the problems involved in berthing in many of the Mediterranean harbours, a problem already touched upon whenever we have mentioned berthing stern-to.

BETTER THAN WATCHING CHRISTIANS BEING FED TO THE LIONS

My most frightening night-mare is the one in which I am berthing *Rolling Wave* in a harbour in the Med. It starts off quite happily. I am trying to insinuate her into the space allocated to me by a sinister-looking harbour official, who speaks no English. Needless to say I have not a smattering of his lingo.

The gap he has allocated to me is between two enormous and expensive gin palaces. Their rails are lined with permanent paid crew members, all of whom are smoking and spitting into the sea. As I am not contributing to their wages they make no attempt to assist.

The gap appears to be about two feet less than *Rolling Wave's* beam.

As it is a Mediterranean harbour the drill is to drop the anchor some distance from the quay, several boat's lengths, in fact, and motor stern-first into the gap, paying out chain as I go, and stopping the boat about three feet from the quay.

There is a strong cross-wind, and several runabouts are belting about the harbour creating washes which send all craft surging and tugging at their warps. A very distinguished looking gentleman, a little like Mr Onassis, appears on the bridge of one yacht. He waves to a lady who resembles Lady Docker, who is standing imperiously on the bridge of the other yacht. They nod to each other. They know what is likely to happen when I start my initial run-in. The permament paid hands know too. They wouldn't miss this for worlds.

At first they are all wrong. I drop the anchor in exactly the right spot; I am lined up stern first in exactly the right direction to compensate for the wind, the washes and the throw of my propeller; the engine is in gear and ticking over at exactly the right number of revs, and I am chucking out exactly the right amount of chain as we go. As we enter the gap it widens miraculously.

There are grudging looks of approval, admiration almost, from the paid hands. Their yachts have twin screws, but they know just how difficult such an operation is with only one screw. Mr Onassis nods benignly. Lady Docker smiles winningly. My stern is now four feet from the quay. I ease the engine into neutral, bound forward and check the boat's way with the cable. Then I bound aft and throw a warp to the sinister-looking harbour official, who takes it, leads it through a ring on the quay and returns the end to me. I make fast. Everything is perfect. The anchor is well dug in and is tending to pull her forward, the warp is just right, we are in no danger of crunching the immaculate sides of the gin palaces, so I stop the engine and run the stern gang plank ashore.

As I step ashore the crowd parts respectfully. The harbour official is waiting for me. We shake hands, and he then indicates by signs that I am in a berth normally reserved for the King of Outer Belgravia. He has been told that the King's yacht has just entered the harbour unexpectedly, I must vacate this berth and take up another one on the other side of the harbour. . .

I assent, bitterly. I take in the gang-plank, and tackle the engine. It is started by swinging by hand and normally it fires first swing, but on this occasion it takes me twenty minutes and by the time it is running I am exhausted. All this time the royal yacht has been circling the harbour and is now flashing rude messages with an Aldis lamp, the harbour official is gibbering with frustration and the permanent paid crew-members are sneering at me openly. They have push-button starting on their boats.

I cast off the stern line and bring it on board. A sudden gust of wind catches *Rolling Wave* and we gently nudge the gin palace on our port hand. I put the engine into forward gear and we slowly move forward. A black smudge from the old tyres we use as fenders smears the immaculate sides of the gin palace. I make a mental note to throw away the tyres and buy proper yacht fenders.

The engine is now in neutral and I leap forward to the winch, insert the handspike into the socket, and start winching in chain. The handspike splits in two and I fall flat on my back on the deck.

The night-mare is now well under way.

Handspike number two is made of sterner stuff, however, and remains intact. I winch feverishly, sweat pouring down my face and completely steaming up my spectacles. Because the hawse pipe is not directly under the gipsy I have to keep tension on the chain, which has already passed over it, with one hand, while I operate the handspike with the other.

As I feed chain down the hawse-pipe a bight drops on my toe. I am barefoot as usual and 5/8 ins chain is heavy stuff. Obviously a toe, maybe two, is broken. I am too busy to be able to stop and find out.

A back eddy of wind now catches our bow and *Rolling Wave* sheers away to starboard. The bowsprit stabs the side of the gin palace on that side and a splintering of wood tells me that either we have stove in a plank on the gin palace, or smashed our bowsprit, or both.

I continue to winch in chain and the bowsprit gouges a great groove down the side of the gin palace. On the bridge Mr Onassis looks unhappy. It is not his gin palace, but he cannot stand incompetence. The paid hands do not look happy either. They know that this means they will have to do some work.

Eventually the chain is straight up and down. I give a mighty two-handed heave on the handspike to break out the anchor and fall flat on my back again. Handspike number two is not made of stern stuff either.

I stagger to my feet. By now I am so exhausted that I can hardly stand. Our stern swings round, caught by the wind, and slams hard into the bow of the other gin palace. The impact smashes our stern light and appears to break out the gin palace's anchor.

Lady Docker looks unhappy. It is not her gin palace, she does not quite understand what is happening, but she knows that things are not usually quite like this.

The wind, freshening all the time, catches the gin palace, and she bashes into the yacht next to her. There is further splintering of wood and then a series of bangs, thuds, crashes and still more splinterings as each yacht in turn breaks out her anchor and crunches into the yacht next door.

Altogether, seventeen yachts of all shapes and sizes, all expensive, thump into each other, like goods wagons in a siding.

The rest of the night-mare is a little confused, but it seems that our anchor is foul of some obstruction on the harbour bed. While taking a stern line back to the quay the harbour official's launch is caught under our stern and sinks. The harbour official has to swim for his life.

In the morning a bill is presented to me. It adds up to £117,999.75. The floating crane used to lift the obstruction on the harbour bed is not man enough for the job, and instead of raising the obstruction pulls itself over and capsizes.

*   *   *

Berthing *a la Med.* is not really quite as bad as this night-mare would lead one to believe: it just sometimes feels like it.

The main thing is to get the anchor down in the right place and to pay out chain at the right speed. You need someone reliable to undertake this chore, because two people are required for the operation in any large-ish boat.

At the same time you have to remember that few single screw yachts will steer when going astern. You therefore have to know how your boat behaves when going backwards and what effect cross-winds are likely to have, and compensate for the two effects. Harbour officials like yachts to be tied up at right angles to the quay and not in echelon, and they will make you do it all over again if you get it wrong first time.

You will have to know how the paddle-wheel effect of suddenly increasing engine revolutions when going astern will swing your stern round, and how much. If you are not lying square to the quay it is often possible to go forward with a stern line on one quarter and pull the boat straight that way. Most yachts have a tighter turning circle when going ahead with the rudder over one way than the other; again due to the throw of the screw.

If you know how your own boat behaves in different

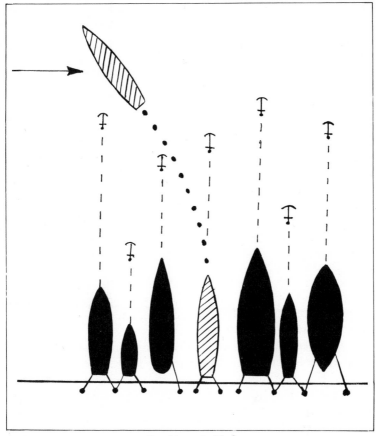

Berthing a la Med.

circumstances you can use the wind or the throw of the
propeller to get you into a tight gap. Often you will find
yourself in a situation where you are down-wind of where
you want to be and unable to get your stern round because it
means steering against the throw of the screw. In this
situation the only thing to do is to motor forward, get in the
anchor, and have another go.

While you are in the middle of doing this you will most
likely become wind-rode, so you will have to haul in the
chain pretty smartly if you are to avoid the kind of crunch
that figures in my night-mares.

This business of paddle-wheeling is worth studying. If you

get the opportunity to watch a fishing boat berthing you will see what can be done by utilising the action of the prop.

Just to watch the fleet coming alongside in a busy port like Ostende or Boulogne is an education in itself. Boats will take one line ashore or onto another boat already alongside and then paddle-wheel into a gap only as long as themselves.

I do not claim advanced skills at berthing stern-to, far from it, but I can turn *Rolling Wave* in virtually her own length — but only to starboard, subject to wind and tide.

Once tied up stern-to, most Mediterranean yachtsmen have a special Med. gangplank which runs from stern to quay, and often these are most elaborate affairs. They feature wheels on the quay so that they move gently back and forwards as the yacht ranges about, and many of them hang in a kind of gimbals system from the after end of the yacht so that up and downwards and sideways movement of the boat is compensated for.

We found that our 12ft scaffold board was perfectly adequate even though harbour officials and Guardia and so on tended to sneer a little on occasion. Only pride persuaded some of the less agile to mount the board at all.

It is quite surprising how often one tends to foul under-water obstructions in harbours in the Med. Often these turn out to be lengths of chain, maybe someone else's cable or just a discarded length. Fortunately the water is often so clear that you can see the nature of the beast with which you have to deal, which makes treatment a whole lot more simple.

If you do get your anchor foul under a length of chain you can usually lift enough of the chain by hauling in the anchor cable to enable you to get a rope or a boat hook under it. Then if you take the weight on to a stout bollard you can lower your own anchor and swing it free. The essence of this operation is speed, because while you are doing it you are at the mercy of wind and current.

This malarkey is another reason for dropping your anchor a good way from the quay. If you do swing while you are sorting yourself out you are less likely to crunch another yacht. The more chain you have out the more the anchor will bite and the greater the length of chain the better it will hold and the stronger the damping effect it will have on surges by the boat.

It is a common sight in the Med. to see someone throw out an anchor shackled on to a length of nylon warp. This kind of thing gives me night-mares too.

BACK TO OUR MUTTONS YET AGAIN!
Still heading south you come to the harbour of Aguilas, the entrance to which is to the right of the ruins of a conspicuous castle. Tie up on the quay to port, stern-to.

Breakers rolling in near Cabo de Gata.

Another twenty-one miles on lies the harbour at Garrucha, which has some facilities for yachts, but which is also a port which owes a large part of its existence to catering for the iron ore mines which are located inland, as indeed do Portman and Escombrera.

Garrucha is the sort of place where the local people will escort you personally to make sure that you really do arrive at the place you enquired after, and by the time you reach your destination you may have acquired a whole train of courteous but inquisitive Spaniards.

By now you are leaving the Costa Blanca and entering the

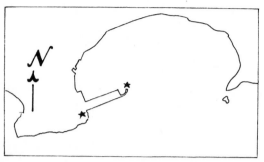

Aguilas

Costa del Sol, well named, because the sun really does beat down, and you begin to understand why the Spanish have that tradition of the siesta. I found it just too hot to work when the sun was high, and if you feel lethargic it is better to admit defeat and go and have a zizz in the shade.

Again this is an essential part of the Dream. What better than to be moored in one of the lonely anchorages, where yours is the only yacht, where probably there is no one else in sight, and where you can dive over the side into that beautiful clear water without bothering about a costume, where you can stay in the water for as long as you like, and

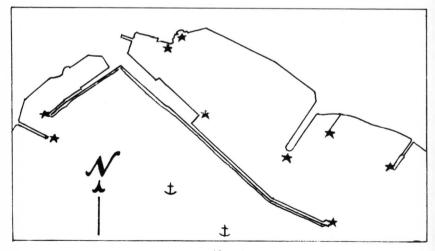

Almeria

A corner of the harbour at Almeria

then relax in the shade until the sun sinks a little lower in the sky and you feel a few spasms of energy creeping back into your system?

The first real harbour in the Costa del Sol is Almeria, about fifty miles from Garrucha. Like Alicante, this is a commercial harbour, and like Alicante the commerce does not intrude too much on the yacht berths, which lie by the *Club Nautico*. If the club does not attract you it is possible to anchor off. The town itself has a smart modern shopping centre, reached by following a palm-tree lined road from the *Club Nautico*.

There are a number of interesting buildings to be seen here, but the best time to go sight-seeing is in the early evening, to dodge the sun.

It is about thirty miles to Adra, the next harbour, which is largely devoted to fishing. The harbour is formed by two sea walls.

A better place for yachts is Motril, about twenty-six miles further on, where you can find a berth at the quay by the

141

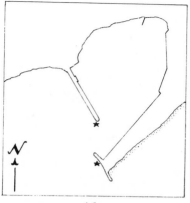

Adra

Club Nautico, or where you can anchor nearby. The town itself lies about a mile away, down a road which runs through fields of sugar cane, and in the town the Moorish influence is reflected in the architectural style of the buildings.

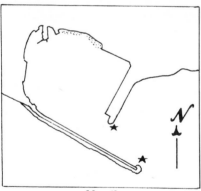

Motril

If you want to get away from the boat for a brief time during the trip this may be the opportunity, because the historic town of Granada is only forty-three miles away and can be reached by road or rail fairly easily. What price a little hitch-hiking and a night in a hotel before hitch-hiking back?

The next harbour down the coast is Almunecar, a fifteen mile passage. Unfortunately its attractions have put it firmly on the tourist map, and you may prefer to go to Malaga, thirty-four miles further on.

There is a well-sheltered harbour at Malaga, and you enter

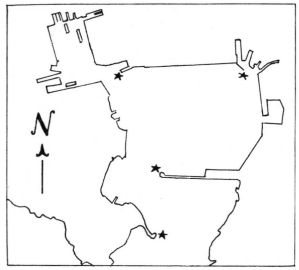

Malaga

between the moles and carry straight on between the next
pair of harbour walls facing you directly ahead, and into the
inner harbour. The *Club Nautico* lies to starboard. They are
not too co-operative here to visiting yachtsmen, perhaps
because one is getting a little too close to Gibraltar for the
political atmosphere not to be felt, but we have been able to
find a berth stern-to on the quay. The area where yachts
moor is open to the swell which sometimes comes right
through the harbour entrance and it can provide an uncomfortable berth.

The harbour is used by large commercial ships, including
liners, and the town itself is attractive and sophisticated. It is
a good place in which to stock up with wine. Take your
five-gallon kegs ashore and find a *bodega* where they serve
from the wood. After a little tasting – for free – you can fill
up the kegs at ridiculously low prices, and if you stagger back
to the yacht it may be largely due to the weight of the kegs!

Malaga has its share of interesting places and museums, and
will be assured of a place in history as the birth-place of
Pablo Picasso.

Just a reminder here that Malaga experiences a slight tidal
flow.

The next harbour is Marbella, about thirty-two miles away,

143

The harbour at Malaga

a small fishing port, another iron-ore centre, and nowadays a tourist centre of note. The best course of action here is to anchor in the middle of the harbour and seek instructions as to a permanent berth at the *Club Nautico.*

Some three-and-a-half miles away is the new marina harbour of Puerto Jose Banus. It is alleged to be the sort of place where they cater for what Mike Peyton has christened the rich, the very rich, and the filthy rich. The marina has a reputation of providing poor service and over-charging overnight visitors.

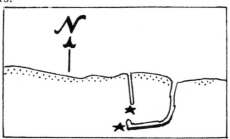

Marbella

The marine parking lot at Puerto Jose Banus. This is just part of it!

The harbour consists of what the developers have described as '38 acres of luxury yacht berths' — or did they mean berths for luxury yachts, or luxury berths for yachts? Everything is laid on, except perhaps humanity and charm. Like so many so-called marina developments it is, to a large extent, an expensive hotel and housing complex with marina facilities as a carrot to attract the investor, to justify planning approval, and distract from its real purpose, which is to make a lot of money for a small number of people.

Having got that off my chest, let us look at Estepona, nineteen miles from Marbella and twenty-two miles from Gibraltar. This is a small fishing port with a small *Club Nautico* where you can lie stern-to, though it is often overcrowded.

Because of its proximity to Gibraltar and the general political situation this is a harbour where one might anticipate a less than welcoming reception from time to time, and it will probably be better on balance to by-pass Estepona and make straight for Gibraltar, a pity as the harbour is charming.

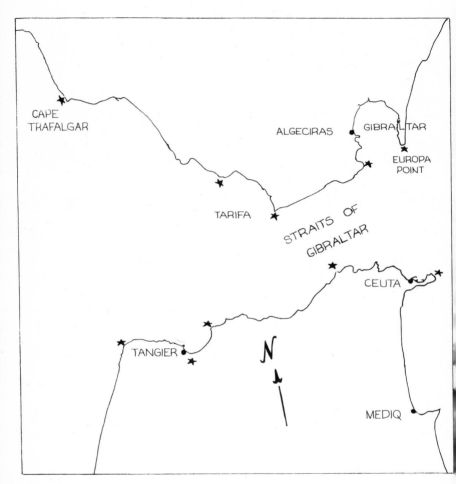

Straits of Gibraltar

5. A Whiff of the Exotic

This section starts off with a few words about Gibraltar, which may make the heading seem a little ill-chosen. Can Gibraltar really be described as exotic? To a large extent I think it can – but first a few words about how to find Gib. and where to tie up.

There is a tidal range of up to six feet at Gib., a factor to take into account when navigating there, and a change after the lack of tides further east. There are strong and erratic currents in the Straits of Gibraltar itself, and there are often winds of some power in the area, so that navigation requires more attention the closer to Gib. you get. It is easier to be set off course here than elsewhere in the Med.

Gibraltar can often be seen from considerable distances, up to thirty miles or more. But the famous Rock is often shrouded in mist and the whole area is prone to fogs, so don't bank on just seeing the Rock from afar and steering on it.

On the eastern side of the rock the great concrete walls of the water catchments reflect the sun and glint brightly and can sometimes be seen when the natural rock itself is obscured.

When you come from the east the harbour is 'round the corner' as it were, and there is a choice of places in which to

Gibraltar from the air (picture: Gibraltar Tourist Office)

berth. By arrangement with the Queen's Harbourmaster you can tie up in what are known as the destroyer pens, which lie to the western end of the part of the harbour which is contained within the moles.

Or you can try to find a vacant berth in the marina, which lies right past the commercial harbour and round the corner, facing the airstrip.

These two locations both cost money. You can anchor for nothing, however, in the area between the airstrip and the marina, and after a short while you will become accustomed to aeroplanes landing and taking off a few yards away. Luckily nothing quite as noisy or monstrous as VC10's or Jumbos fly to Gib.

Apart from the inconvenience of having to row ashore there is nothing wrong with anchoring, (except when the winds do blow,) and this is what I would suggest you do.

Gibraltar itself is an odd place, rather like a cross between Aldershot and Chatham at the time of Queen Victoria, inhabited by a mixture of Ugandan Indians, provincial British and anglicised Spanish. There are also a lot of Moroccans, who have replaced the cheap Spanish labour which can no longer work in Gib. since the frontier was closed.

There seem to be more cars per yard of road than anywhere else in Europe and because of the closing of the frontier there is really nowhere for them to go.

The people of Gibraltar are the most patriotic people in the world. I have never ever seen, anywhere else, PRO-British slogans painted on walls.

The town itself is really just a large village perched on the side of a very steep hill, and if your time at sea has accustomed you to the wide open spaces you may find Gibraltar a little claustrophobic.

There is a lot of fascinating history attached to Gib., and although the cemetery which contains the bodies of British troops and seamen dating back as far as Trafalgar is at the level of Main Street, to capture most of the historical atmosphere of Gib. you have to go climbing. It is well worth making the pilgrimage to the top of the Rock and well worth finding the famous apes.

Gibraltar is a duty-free port, which means that you can

The light-house at Europa Point, Gibraltar
(picture: Gibraltar Tourist Office)

stock up with cheap booze and cigarettes better here than anywhere else you visit, but the prices of virtually everything else in the shops are higher than in Great Britain as a direct result of its enforced insularity. Everything has to be imported.

There are a number of shops in Main Street which cater for the cruise liner passengers and they have comprehensive stocks of electronic gear like transistor radios, TV sets, hi fi sets, tape recorders and the rest of the electronic equipment which so many people find so necessary to support life. The prices are way above what they should be in a duty free port. Most of the shop-keepers are Indian and it is hard to believe that they intend to sell anything without a protracted bout of bazaar-style negotiation.

Is Gibraltar exotic? You will judge for yourself, but to my mind much of it is exotic in a funny sort of uniquely Gibraltar way.

While you are at Gib. it is a good idea to check up on how you are doing against your itinerary. How much money have you left? Is it lasting as well as you anticipated? How much tinned stuff have you left in stock?

How are you making out as far as time is concerned? Are you still within your schedule?

One of the odd things about Gib. is that so many long distance voyages seem to fail here. If you tie up in the destroyer pens or in the marina you will probably receive a constant stream of young men and women of all nationalities asking if you want to hire crew. Many are from round-the-world yachts which got no further than Gib.

Perhaps the money ran out, perhaps the boat turned out to be unseaworthy, perhaps after the passage of enough time to enable the yacht to reach Gib. the nerves of the crew became frayed as a result of living for a long period in a confined space with people with whom they were basically incompatible. But for whatever reason, there is no shortage of experienced crew offering their services.

They will be happy to help work your boat in return for a bed, food, and beer money. Many sleep on the beach in the summer until something turns up for them. Some have had to sell their yacht to get themselves out of debt. Their presence offers a tacit warning that unless you have planned your trip properly and work your plan — you could end up as one of them.

This is why it is wise to check out your finances and the time available to you while you are at Gib. Assuming the money is lasting out you have several options.

- You can turn round and go back to Agde and the Canal du Midi.
- You can make for home round the coast of Portugal.
- You can make a detour to Tangier and then make for home by either route
- You can hop over to the Balearics and then make for home via Agde and the Canal du Midi.
- You can head for France/Italy/Corsica/Greece, wherever you choose.

Gib. is one of the world's cross-roads. Don't be surprised if you bump into someone you know at Gib: it is like the underground at Piccadilly Circus in that respect.

If you can manage it you should cross the Straits to Tangier. With its evil reputation, and evil and fascinating reality you will be delighted that you took your yacht there while the opportunity presented itself, and if you don't you will regret it for a long time afterwards.

The passage to Tangier shouldn't take you more than half a day, despite tide rips, currents, *Vendevales, Levanters,* fogs, shipping and the general trickiness of navigation in the Straits of Gibraltar.

In the harbour at Tangier you can either seek a berth at the yacht club or tie up to the outer wall on the starboard hand as you enter, where there usually are a number of other yachts.

Wherever you elect to stay remember that the rich Tangier reputation includes some strong hints that every item of equipment on a yacht, including the mast and engine, particularly the mast and engine in fact, will disappear like lightning the moment your back is turned, unless they are nailed down with six-inch nails and padlocked as well. Light objects like echo-sounders and boat hooks just go by some mysterious oriental process of levitation.

The solution to this problem is to employ a ship-keeper as watchman. Then if anything goes you know that it was him because he will fight off all his friends on your behalf.

Finding such a person is easy, because when you tie up you are likely to be challenged imperiously about your lack of courtesy in not wearing a large Moroccan courtesy flag, and then the challenger will promptly offer to sell you one for whatever sum of money he thinks you will tolerate. This is the man who may well turn out to be your friendly neighbourhood ship-keeper during your stay.

Strike a bargain with him, don't allow him on board, return unexpectedly several times during the first day or so, pay him daily so that he can see that you are honouring your part of the bargain, refuse all offers of hash, if you must take a taxi select the one the ship-keeper's friend drives, and probably all will end well and nothing will be stolen.

Your ship-keeper will fight off the thieves valiantly on your behalf. He knows who they are, of course, most are his friends or relatives.

In the town itself make your way to the Tourist Office where they will be able to give you a map showing the location of all the interesting places, from the Casbah to the Soccos, and with its aid you will be able to see a great deal of Tangier without having to employ one of the guides who will pester you during your entire stay, wherever you go. If you do decide to employ a guide take one recommended to you by, guess whom, your friendly neighbourhood ship-keeper.

Tangier can be a good place in which to buy souvenirs and presents for Aunt Mabel in Brighton, providing you don't pay anything like the asking prices.

Sample dialogue between the author and a shopkeeper:
Harper. 'How much is that leather pouffe cover?'
Shop-keeper. 'Ten Pounds Sair.'
Harper. 'Ten Pounds! I wouldn't give you thirty bob for it!'
Shop-keeper. 'Done Sair.'
Wife. 'What is that brown paper parcel under your arm? What happened?'
Harper. (Bitterly). 'I don't know.'

Another recommended activity at Tangier is to take a bus ride, where to is not important. We have found that this is nearly always a good way to get to know a country and to absorb its atmosphere. People in buses are the ones who live there, they are going about their business as people, and they are not as worldly or sophisticated or affluent as the people who travel in cars. There is no tourist 'front' or gimmickry, and buses take people from real place to real place, not to somewhere dreamed up by the tourist board or the entrepreneurs who supply tourists with what they think the tourists should have.

So take a bus in Tangier, though the experience may make you feel that there is something a little wrong with a world in which so few have so much and so many have so little.

Another thing about Tangier is that it seems as if half the population is hooked on some form of drug, hash, opium, or what have you. If someone offers you the makings of a cigarette be prepared for what they really are. And if you want to be convinced of the evils of the drug traffic just keep your eyes open and watch out for the attractive youngsters of both sexes who have come to Tangier from Europe just to be able to obtain drugs easily. They are hooked to the exclusion of everything else in the world.

Sit in a street cafe for an hour with a glass of mint tea, (which is delicious, and almost compensates for the fact that being a Moslem country, alcoholic refreshment is not as readily obtainable as in Europe,) and watch the passing scene. Clapham will never be the same again.

The prevailing winds in Tangier are unfavourable for leaving the place, and people tell dismal stories about being there for weeks, waiting for a wind change which would enable them to cross back over the Straits to Europe. . . .

We found that by leaving at four in the morning we were able to motor out into the Bay of Tangier and escape the wind 'prison' before it reached its full strength.

Before we left we had to waken our trusty friendly neighbourhood ship-keeper from a drug-induced sleep (he sleeps in his peaked dual-purpose taxi-drivers/yachting cap) in order to pay him. A little to his surprise I feel.

A headland near Ceuta (picture: Gibraltar Tourist Office)

If you want to see a little more of North Africa before you leave it you can make for Ceuta, which lies some thirty miles to the east, or keep on and go round the corner to M'diq, another twenty-five miles further on.

Ceuta is an ancient walled city, full of history, while at M'diq there is a brand new harbour, so new that when we visited it the Admiralty Chart still insisted that it was an anchorage. M'diq — also spelled Mediq, M'dik. Medik, and several other permutations on the theme, is the place where we saw a lady sunbathing in a bikini on the beach protecting her modesty by retaining her yashmak.

Apart from Ceuta and M'diq there is really no other place worth making for in the part of North Africa within reasonable reach, so you will probably want to return to Gibraltar or perhaps Estepona or one of the other Spanish ports.

Gibraltar lies virtually due north of Ceuta and M'diq and well to the east of Tangier, another reason for making the detour to one of these two ports before heading back towards Europe. The prevailing winds and currents are by no means as unfavourable as from Tangier, though the currents in the Straits area can behave with such a complete lack of predictability that you may make good a very different course from what you intended.

I am still working on the assumption that you have to continue to watch expenditure like a hawk but want to make another detour to the Balearics if you possibly can, and still have enough time in hand to enable you to do so.

If you have been to Gibraltar already it is best to make your arrival port in Spain as far away as possible, to avoid the possible nastiness which the present political situation can create at petty officialdom level ·for any one who has just come from Gib. The degree of nastiness is in direct proportion to the proximity to Gib. itself, so it would be better to make for Malaga or for the Balearics direct, although this is quite a long haul.

Should you go back to Gib. and then on to Malaga you can always tell the officials there that in fact you have just come from Ceuta or M'diq, producing your passport to prove it. From then on it's up the Spanish coast, calling at either the

You want a camel ride? This may be you opportunity! M'diq, the hills of Cabo Negro in the background. (picture: Jonathan Eastland)

places you missed out on the way down or at the places you liked best.

Before starting to discuss the Balearics perhaps it would be a good idea to mention a few things relevant to yachting in Spanish waters.

THE NATIVES ARE ALWAYS FRIENDLY

The first thing is water. Drinking water, that is. What comes out of the taps in Spanish harbours is not always of a standard to which we are accustomed in England, even if the tap is marked 'potable'. This is particularly true in the southern half of Spain, where rain water is often collected in roof tanks and then finds its way into the drinking water system.

The remedy is to fill up whenever you are sure that the water on offer really is good, and the advice of a Spaniard of the professional classes is worth taking on this point rather than a fisherman, whose natural courtesy is such that he will tell you the water is OK rather than upset you by telling you to the contrary if he believes that you want to be told that it is OK, if you see what I mean.

In addition, the use of the little pills which the multiple chemists sell to sterilise water is of benefit.

It helps, too, if you have a seperate water tank for drinking water only, which is never tapped for washing or any other purpose. This tank is only ever filled with water of guaranteed purity.

Club Nauticos have been mentioned a few times so far. They are nothing like UK yacht clubs, they are really social clubs where business men gather because it is a smart place to eat or do business. Many of the members do not have a boat and would run a mile rather than go out in one.

Club Nauticos are the places where they dress for dinner, rather than guzzle sandwiches and slurp beer at the bar, clad in wet jeans and an anorak.

They are thus usually, expensive and do not welcome the impecunious.

We have already mentioned that awnings are pretty essential items of yachting equipment in the southern parts of the Med. and that the sun can have a debilitating effect on someone accustomed to the vagaries of the weather in the

UK. You will also find that paint and varnish, the latter especially, do not like too much sun either, and that weed and marine growth generally flourish in the hot water area along the water-line.

Anti-fouling has a much tougher time in the Med. Most yachtsmen who keep their boats there all the year round eventually scrap the idea of varnish, and paint everything. I am not suggesting that you do this, but be prepared for a lot of catching up when you get home and if you can haul out and scrub the bottom while you are in the Med. it will be worth the effort.

I suggest, too, that you paint the waterline with an anti-fouling boot-topping. These are wildly expensive per pint, but a pint does go a very long way, and the paint is effective, so the actual cost in use is not really as bad as it seems at first.

When you arrive in any Spanish harbour the Civil Guard are among the first people to pay attention to you, and very often they will be waiting for you to tie up. With their funny hats and carbines they are often rather sinister figures. All they want you to do is to fill in their forms and once you have done this they will usually depart quite amicably. So don't be alarmed. If you are friendly to them they will be friendly back. They all smoke, especially on duty, and Freeman's is their favourite brand!

One night we anchored off a popular tourist resort and ignored the two members of the Guardia waiting for us on the beach and ignored, too, their signals that we should come ashore to fill in the forms. Night fell and the glow-worms in the dark as they puffed their cigarettes showed that they were still there. When we went to bed they were still waiting for us. An hour later a bump on the side of the boat indicated that we had visitors. Slightly alarmed I scrambled up to see what it was – surely they hadn't swum out, or sent a Guardia gun-boat?

To our relief we were hailed by two Australians from a pedallo, one of the fibre glass boats which are propelled by the crew pedalling like a bicycle. These two waved the magic form in the light of their torch and explained that the

Guardia had blackmailed them into coming out to see us by talking about their bar-tender's work permits coming up for renewal and would they like to co-operate by . . . The arm of the Guardia is a long one.

One of the nice things about trips of the kind we deal with in this book is when your mail finally catches up with you. A great big packet of mail, and hardly a bill among them, it's almost like being back in the Forces!

The thing here is that not all Spanish post offices are terribly efficient when it comes to operating the *poste restante* system, and they are unlikely to forward your mail. So give your friends only a few places, with deadlines for mailing to each, as much as three weeks before you *expect* to leave them, and nominate as the principal place a large town which you are likely to visit more than once. If you can nominate Gibraltar as one place it is a good thing because there at least there are no language problems in sorting things out with the counter staff.

Obviously things change from time to time, in the political world, but as I have said, it is as well to remember when cruising in Spanish waters that the official Spanish attitude is that Gib. is part of Spain, and there are times when yachts-men who are just going there or have just come back from it may find that officialdom is less than helpful. This is par-ticularly true in harbours near to the Rock itself, and it manifested itself in a rather unpleasant fashion when we anchored in a bay not so many miles from that controversial peninsula. We made friends with some people who lived in the small village on the water's edge, and were all set to row ashore and have dinner with them, and in fact got as far as the quay. Here the Guardia refused to allow us ashore on the grounds that we had not been cleared or did not have the necessary visa or permit or whatever. Next day we were asked ashore again to go shopping by our new friends, who were hopping mad about the whole thing, and had made a big issue with the Guardia that we would starve unless we were allowed into the village to buy bread — so into the village we went, solemnly escorted by the Guardia, to buy bread which we didn't want!

Let us leave this section on a happier note. One of the

delights of cruising in these waters is the presence of dolphins and flying fish.

Dolphins are beautiful creatures, who seem to have some means of communicating with human beings. At all events, we always knew when there were dolphins about minutes before they actually broke surface and swam up to say hello to us. They travel in pairs and trios and schools, and seem to come up to a yacht just to see what you look like, perform a few tricks for you like sounding and diving in concert and then set off again on their own business.

Flying fish flash in the sun, rarely, but beautifully banking and swerving to avoid waves until they splash back into their more natural element again.

Dolphins and flying fish, two more essential ingredients in the Dream. A further one is the way you make friends with the other cruising yachtsmen you meet on your travels.

If you are prepared to take them on their face value, as they will take you, you will meet and make friends with an awful lot of nice people of both sexes and various nationalities all the time you are wandering around the Med.

Some may become good lifelong friends in the true sense of the word. You will find that you have a lot in common with people who have a few words of English — for most foreigners do — and whose language you cannot begin to understand. You may have entirely different backgrounds and experiences, you may be superficially very different, have widely differing incomes, but there will so often be that unspoken camaraderie which is priceless and virtually unique, and a part of the Dream which you will long treasure when you have forgotten which port was which.

Or so I have found.

RETURNING TO OUR MUTTONS FOR VERY NEARLY THE LAST TIME

So you are now retracing your steps back up the Spanish coast with a run over to the Balearics in mind.

The shortest passage is from a sheltered rocky cove at a place called Morayra, near Cap Nao, north of Alicante. It is about sixty miles from here to the island of Ibiza. If you can find it there is a perfect tranquil anchorage on Ibiza at a

A corner of the harbour at Ibiza (picture: Spanish Tourist Office)

place called Cala Yondal on the south side of the island. You
may be lucky enough to be able to spend several days here
undisturbed by the arrival of other boats and with scarcely a
sign of human activity on the shore. The swimming in the
crystal clear water is superb and you can watch the inquisi-

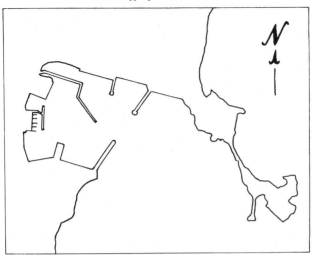

Ibiza harbour

tive bright blue little fish examining your anchor or you can just relax in the sun.

Eventually the necessity to buy fresh food or take on water will lead you on. There are two recognised harbours on the island of Ibiza, the first being the port of Ibiza itself, rapidly becoming one of the more unpleasant tourist resorts, which has had a 'hippy problem' in years gone by. Since long hair, beards and bare feet are not the exclusive property of hippies there may be the problem of being confused with them yourself and thus running foul of the Guardia. As an additional factor the tourist-orientation of the place may result in Ibiza town having little appeal for you.

If you do decide to go there, however, yachts tie up at the *Club Nautico,* which lies directly ahead when you pass between the sea walls which secure the harbour.

The alternative harbour on Ibiza is San Antonio, on the northern side of the island. Here, too, the mighty tourist is well catered for, and what was once a small fishing harbour is now the largest resort on the island. When you enter the harbour you pass round the sea wall and tie up stern-to among the other yachts on the quay facing you.

There is another small island in the Balearic group, little known until quite recently, and one of the most enchanted places you will visit on your trip.

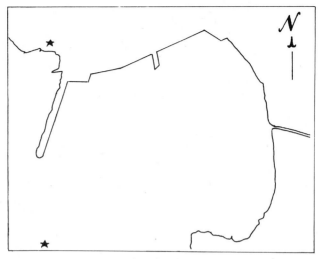

San Antonio

This is the island of Espalmador, a real Robinson Crusoe place, and a short passage from Cala Yondal. You anchor here in a bay which resembles nothing so much as a south seas atoll. The bay is largely land-locked, the beaches are silver sand, and the vegetation of the island, which is quite small, is semi-tropical in appearance. As you enter you could believe that you were going into a secluded bay in the Bahamas.

The island is privately owned, but the owner is completely tolerant towards the yachts which visit his little paradise, and in return the yachtsmen respect the fact that they are really trespassing. If you do go ashore to explore keep away from the house, and follow the example of the other visitors and take your litter away from the island with you.

At the week-end a surprisingly large number of expensive gin-palaces arrive at high speed from the Spanish mainland, complete with paid crew to attend to the needs of the owners and their friends, who normally include a few dolly-birds as part of the creature comforts without which their lives would be incomplete.

Happily, these people, too, respect the beauties of the island and the presence of other yachtsmen, and it is a rare thing at Espalmador to hear a loud transistor radio. Nude bathing is becoming popular here, and indeed, why not?

Espalmador is one of the 'must' places for your list. But don't attempt to enter at night because the entrance is unlit.

The island of Formentera is only a short distance from Ibiza and Espalmador, and the only harbour, at Cala Sabina, may be an essential call for water and fresh food. Prices are high here, because like all the Balearics, nearly everything has to be imported from the mainland, including even the drinking water.

The harbour is not one which has any appeal for me, and it may be better in good weather to anchor a short distance off the beach a few hundred yards short of the harbour and row ashore. The sea here is a gorgeous turquoise colour.

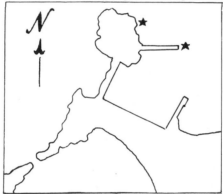

Formentera

A characteristic of the Balearics is that there are numerous small bays and coves which make ideal anchorages though the chart would not lead you to suppose so. To find them and take advantage of them is part of the Dream.

You will almost certainly want to visit Mallorca before you start for home. The distance from Ibiza to Mallorca is about fifty-five miles, and a good jumping off point is Cala San Vicente, on the north eastern tip of Ibiza. You can make for either Port Andraitx or Palma itself.

The former is to be preferred if you don't want to be swamped by the tourist activity which is concentrated at Palma. At Andraitx, the tourists seem to arrive by coach and leave the same way for their hotels elsewhere, without becoming too much part of the landscape.

You enter Andraitx by leaving the first breakwater to port

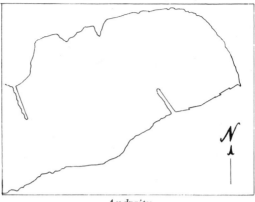

Andraitx

and the second to starboard, and then anchoring clear of the fairway, or in the outer half of the harbour before you get too near to the second breakwater. Alternatively, you can tie up among other yachts at the second breakwater, though this can be a noisy place at night.

The anchorage is a good one except in very heavy winds, which can funnel down the mountains, and in fact we have dragged here.

The harbour at Palma is only a short run from Andraitx. It is used by a large number of big commercial craft, the town itself is a flourishing one, largely devoted, it appears, to the jaundiced eye, to taking money off tourists.

You enter by leaving the long, angled sea wall to port and making for the short straight wall which lies to starboard. Once round this you can see the very large – and expensive – marina to your right. The first night's stay was free when I was there last, and thereafter a berth costs the earth. It may be worth it even so, to take advantage of the water stand pipes on the pontoons.

You can anchor in the harbour for nothing, however, in the area between the marina and the boulevard which runs along the harbour. Anchor fairly close in so that you don't have too far to row when you go ashore and so that you are clear of the path taken by the fishing boats which use the harbour.

The disadvantage of anchoring too close in is that the music, so-called, from the discotheque on the shore is belted out at an incredible decibelular rate until about four in the morning and will keep most people awake until dawn.

Palma is a good place in which to go shopping. It boasts a covered market where food is cheaper than in the shops. The Shell credit scheme applies in Palma. To organise things you have to walk to Puerto Pi at the other end of the harbour, near the shipyard, to where the offices of the fuel people are situated. In Spain the supply of diesel fuel is a state monopoly, which means that a certain amount of beaurocratic formality has to be completed. However, the scheme does work.

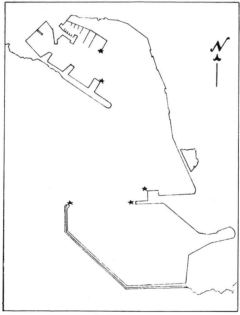

Palma

The island of Mallorca does boast other harbours, seven recognised ones, starting with Porto Petro, most attractive, on the east side. Porto Colom lies to the north and is unattractive, there is Porto Cristo further north and unattractive also. The next harbour up is Cala Ratjada, an unspoilt fishing harbour which is off the beaten track for tourists. You should be able to find a berth here to starboard after you have passed the end of the sea wall, among the other yachts, after the fishing boats. Puerto Alcidia lies further north again and is a declining fishing port with a share of the tourist trade and some industry.

The Club Nautico at Palma, Mallorca. You won't be welcome here in your swimming costume only.

Tucked away round the corner is Puerto Pollensa, one haven you will probably want to visit. Here you tie up to port once you have passed between the moles. There is quite a lot of tourist activity at Puerto Pollensa.

This leaves one harbour, Soller, on the north west of the island. Soller is attractive, even though a naval base is located here. You will see this to port as you enter the harbour. Yachts tie up stern-to at a short cross jetty at the end of a quay which juts out into the harbour.

There is a rather splendid tramway at Soller, which is also something of a hazard to pedestrians who may be a little unused to such things if they have just stepped off a yacht.

The Balearics include another large island, Menorca, which lies about forty miles to the north east of Mallorca, and here the most likely harbour to make for after crossing from Mallorca is Ciudadela. This is a long narrow bay with deep water in the middle, and the quays are located towards the bottom end to starboard.

Menorca boasts another harbour, a famous one, Port Mahon, pronounced Mahn, said to be the most beautiful in the whole of the Mediterranean. Nelson's fleets were based here at one time, and there is a small distillery overlooking the harbour where they still make a type of gin which is named 'Lord Nelson' after the great Admiral himself. In taste it reminds one of some of the Dutch gins, and is drunk in the same way, neat — gulp — blimey, just like that. The formula is said to have been handed down intact from the days of Nelson, and after drinking it one can understand why his sailors fought so well in the bloody naval engagements of the time. A few tots of this stuff and you would take on anybody.

Port Mahon is another long narrow bay with deep water all the way. Just follow it until you come to the yacht moorings.

An essential part of the Dream is to cruise among the Balearics for a while. It really is a most beautiful area, with the sun and the sea — two of the vital ingredients of the Dream — at their best. There are plenty of places in which to anchor away from tourism and out of sight of the hotels, and yet you are near enough to the amenities of civilisation to be

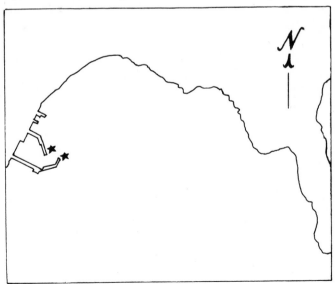

Pollensa

able to get a doctor or dentist in emergency, to buy food and water when necessary, without exposing yourself too much to the tourist resorts.

A secret anchorage on the island of Menorca.

It is therefore all the harder to have to make the final decision to turn for home from the Balearics. Just another week, you will find yourself saying to yourself, and you will rationalise like mad to justify taking it. You will also find yourself trying frantically to find some means of earning a living in the Balearics.

If you can find such a way out of the rat race – take it!

Providing none of your responsibilities at home are so pressing that they cannot be evaded, of course.

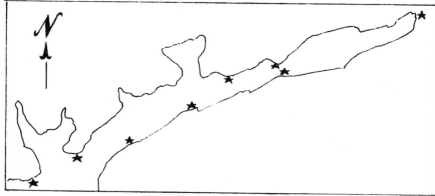

The harbour at Ciudadela, Menorca.

But it won't be easy to find a way of earning a living on any permanent basis. Spanish laws are geared to providing work for their own nationals and preventing foreigners from taking work away from them.

So the chances are that while you are cruising the Balearics you will have to make another realistic assessment about just how long it is going to take you to get back to your own home port.

Remember that October is the time of the equinoctial gales, that you will have to pass through the top part of the Bay of Biscay, that fogs are very common in the Brittany area in the autumn, that there is a limit to the number of locks you can work in a day, and give yourself enough time to get back home again in one piece allowing for delays due to bad weather, engine breakdown and gear failure.

6. Beginning of the Long Trek Home

From which port to which port will you make the first leg of your homeward passage? This depends entirely on you, of course, where you are, when you turn your bows to the north, how long you want to make your 'legs', whether or not there is any port on the way back which you missed on the outward leg because it seemed a good idea to save it up for the homeward stretch, and so on.

It is a little over 100 miles to Barcelona from Pollensa, Mallorca, or Ciudadela on Menorca. From Barcelona you have the run up the coast, into the Golfe de Lyons, until you enter the Canal du Midi at whichever harbour you have selected, Sète, Agde or La Nouvelle.

There is another possibility for boats with plenty of power. This is to go back the way you came, up the Rhône. Your experiences on the way down will have been enough to let you know if this is a practical possibility or not, or whether the current could be so strong that you would be unable to make enough way against for it to be a feasible proposition. The advantage is that this is a quicker and more direct route than going via the Canal du Midi, and it avoids all the problems of navigation and seamanship which the passage from Bordeaux across the Bay of Biscay involves. A tow can

171

be arranged up the Rhône if the worst comes to the worst.

And after you get past Lyons you have the choice of three routes to Paris, so you may not have to retrace your steps completely.

But it would be a tremendous loss to miss the Canal du Midi, and even if you started on the trip a little short of experience, by now you will have gained enough knowledge to be able to cope with the tenser situations you will meet in the Bay of Biscay and the Brittany area.

Each of the possible ways into the Canal du Midi allows passage for boats up to 98ft 5ins long, with a beam of 17ft. 1in. Air heights and depths differ, however. To confuse matters different authorities give different figures, which is less than helpful to an owner who is not sure whether or not he is going to squeeze through by the odd inch.

This is why I suggest that you measure the entrance to the canal at Agde.

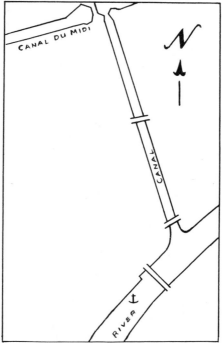

*The cut which connects the River Hérault
with the round lock on the Canal du Midi.*

The river and the main bridge at Agde. The cut for the Canal du Midi is a little way past this bridge to port. (picture : Hugh McKnight)

For what it is worth the following is a guide:-

From Agde	From Sète	From La Nouvelle	
11ft 4ins	11ft 8ins	10ft 7ins	Height under bridges
4ft 9ins	5ft 3ins	5ft 9ins	Depth of Water

The short branch from Agde, on the River Hêrault, runs into a circular lock with three entrances. The one on your left leads into the Canal du Midi proper, the one on the right is for traffic from Sète which will already have passed through two locks on the way from Les Onglous.

A realistic minimum depth in the Canal du Midi is 5ft 3ins although some authorities do claim more. When we went through this is what we drew and I don't think we touched bottom except when we strayed from the channel.

Clearance under the bridges is about 11ft 3ins, but this is at the centre, and many of the bridges are hump-backed, falling away to 7 ft 6 ins at the sides.

The actual headroom and depth depend to a degree on the amount of rainfall there has been recently, and if the water level is low there is a compensating increase in head room.

It is possible to reduce your draught a little by redistributing some of the heavier weights. Most yachts draw more

A pair of local fishing boats running down the cut from Agde and the Canal du Midi. (picture: Hugh McKnight)

aft than forward, so bringing forward as far as possible things like kedge anchor as well as main anchor, engine spares, tool boxes, spare calor gas cylinders, jerricans full of water, and so on, can reduce the draught aft by an inch or so.

In emergency it is sometimes possible to do as Roger Pilkington did and shanghai a load of school children whose combined weights distributed along the length of the boat can lower her just enough to get under a critical bridge!

When we entered the canal at Agde I lowered the masts and brought them both as far forward as possible, and this plus the weight of several jerricans of fuel also brought forward reduced our draft aft from 5ft 6ins to 5ft 3ins. Careful calculations about fuel consumption enabled us to have only just enough fuel on board to get us to Bordeaux, where the trusty Shell Credit Scheme operates. Keeping the bilges pumped also helped, because bilge water tends to run towards the stern and thus lower it. Motoring at slow speeds also assisted because *Rolling Wave,* like many yachts, drops her stern at any speed.

The round lock at the junction of the cut from Agde and the Canal du Midi. (picture: Hugh McKnight)

If you have a mast to strike it is probably best to enter the Canal du Midi at Sète, where there are port facilities and a marina, and therefore cranes with which to do the job.

Assuming that you enter the system at Agde, the cut into the Canal du Midi is located a short distance to port after the stone bridge which carries the heavy traffic of Agde from one bank of the river to the other.

There is one lock, at Toulouse, where the canal passes under a road. Here the lock-keeper may have to juggle with the level of water to make sure that there is depth enough to float you over the sill but not so much that you jam under the bridge.

You could make doubly sure of the clearance under the bridges, if you are in doubt, by following the tow-path from Agde and making scale drawings of the bridges by measurement. There are two different types of standard bridge on the Canal du Midi, the hump-backed ones dating back to the time of the canal's construction, – the ones which cause all the trouble – all built to the same design and therefore identical, and the horizontal concrete ones which are modern, and which should create no problems.

If your scale drawing superimposed on a drawing of the boat to the same scale shows you aren't going to make it you may have to consider drastic surgery like sawing off the top of the wheelhouse and replacing it when you get to Bordeaux. This is by no means unheard of!

The Canal Latéral a la Garonne, which runs from Toulouse to Bordeaux, is deeper and offers better clearances under the bridges than the Canal du Midi.

Having made the Canal du Midi sound more of a hazard than the Rhône, deliberately, to stress that it does have less water and less headroom than the canals on the way down through France, it is high time to redress the balance by under-lining that it is a most beautiful waterway.

Up to the middle of the seventeenth century there was a link by water from Bordeaux to Toulouse, down the river. This was not the easiest of rivers to negotiate, but it was done, using rafts, and by the time cargo had reached Toulouse it was well on its way to the Med. It only needed a water link from Toulouse to the Mediterranean to enable cargoes to be taken overland all the way to the Med. without having to be re-shipped on the backs of mules and horses for the last part of the journey.

If a canal could be cut from Toulouse — a distance of 150 miles — it meant that no cargo need be taken on the long haul round the Iberian Peninsula, and a hazardous sea voyage would be eliminated.

The famous Paul Riquet started construction of a trial canal in 1662 and work on the canal itself was begun in 1667. It was opened in 1681, a few months after the death of Riquet, whose memorial can be seen in the cathedral at Toulouse.

The Canal du Midi is characterised by the elliptical locks, the graceful bridges, and the trees which line both banks so that the horses which towed the barges would be working in the shade. These trees are there still, in their maturity, so that the canal is a cool oasis running in the shade while the sun beats down on either hand.

Canal du Midi. The plane trees provide a welcome shade along its entire length.
(picture: Hugh McKnight)

The channel follows the contours of the land, so that it winds frequently, often with very tight corners. The barges seem to negotiate these without too much trouble, incredibly in view of their length and beam, but you may well find that a sudden unexpected turn of well over 90 degrees will put you up the canal bank if you aren't alert. On some of these corners you may have to pole round or even go astern and make two attempts at it.

The towpath usually passes under the bridges, which results in a knuckle to one side of the channel under the bridge, which in turn means that the centre of the curve of the arch is off the centre line of the canal, a fact to be borne in mind if clearance is tight.

The first part of the canal, from Sète, runs through marshes which are the breeding ground for mosquitoes, and you must take precautions, even though it will be late summer or early autumn when you are in the area. These little beasts breed a long way further north, and repellent creams and treatment are essential.

A three-lock staircase. Note the sill at the bottom of the gates.
(picture: Hugh McKnight)

The Canal du Midi has an atmosphere all its own, tranquil, peaceful, timeless, and the lock-keepers, aware that commercial traffic is steadily declining and that their future is linked to the increase in yachting traffic, are most helpful, charming, courteous and kind.

The first three locks present no problems other than the evolving of a drill which puts your crew ashore on the bank

What happens when the sluices are opened in this lock and the water thunders in.
(picture: Hugh McKnight)

opposite the lock-keeper's house, so that between you the work of operating the sluices and gates is shared. The elliptical shape of the locks present few problems once you get used to it and sort out which set of bollards to use.

You may well decide to stop for the night after the third lock, because the next stretch is going to keep you busy. It starts off with the double lock at Beziers, consisting of two basins with a gate between, so that for the price of working three gates you pass through two locks, a saving in effort which is repeated many times on the Canal du Midi. In these double locks you must pass into the first chamber and raise the level of the water to that of the upper basin before you attempt to enter it, because otherwise you are liable to ram the sill which separates the chambers.

After passing through the port of Beziers you ascend a second double lock, and then it is only a little over a mile before you enter the famous staircase at Fonserannes. Here

The beginning of the seven-lock staircase at Fonserannes.
(picture: Hugh McKnight)

there are no less than seven connected chambers, luckily now electrified. You seem to just go on up and up and up! Confer with the lock-keeper before you start to make sure that you don't land yourself in an impossible situation like you being half way up and meeting a barge which is half way down!

After the staircase there is a nice long uninterrupted run of thirty-four miles without a lock, time in which to get your breath back after Fonserannes. The canal continues to meander like a drunken cow, however, with blind corners and blind bridges and the occasional barge hammering away through the night trying to make up lost time.

While you are under way you really need a look-out up in the bow trying to see the bow of the barge coming towards you round the blind corners.

At Le Malpas you pass through a tunnel, less than 200 yards in length, and posing no problems because you can see if any other craft is approaching from the other direction before you attempt the tunnel yourself. The tunnel is larger than the bridge holes, so there is no problem of height or width.

There are also a couple of one-way sections, which are just over a mile in length, a mile and a quarter after the staircase at Fonserannes.

The acute bends on the Canal du Midi and the inevitability of having to slow down if you are in a largish craft means that it is impossible to belt through the thirty-four mile lock-less stretch and save time. Speed is restricted anyway.

But why try to create records? The canal is far too beautiful and too essential an ingredient in the Dream to squander by hurrying.

And so the canal continues its erratic way, until after another eighty-four locks you reach Toulouse. Many of the locks are two-ers, some are three-ers. There is even a four-er. The canal passes over aqueducts and there is a summit level at 630 feet, which you reach after the Ecluse de la Mediterrané.

At some of the locks you may be offered water – the chances are that it will be well-water. There is good potable tap water available at Homs, however.

Two towns on the route, well worth devoting a little time to exploring, are Carcassone and Castelnaudary.

Carcassone boasts a splendid castle, while at Castelnaudary there is a mediaeval walled city in extremely good repair: not to be missed.

Carcassone is also etched indelibly in my memory as the place where we set off to buy a gallon of paraffin and were directed to a pharmacist. His expression when we asked for what was apparently a gallon of surgical paraffin gave us the clue that we were on the wrong track. Paraffin for oil lamps and Tilley lights is *petrole Kerdane.* Tilley spares, including wicks, are not too easily obtained on the Continent, incidentally, it is best to take a good stock of mantles with you.

Finally you arrive at Toulouse, where the canal enters a large octagonal basin where barges congregate and one of the hire cruiser operators has a base. It is easy to find a berth in the basin and leave the boat while you spend a day exploring the town. In addition to its fame as the centre of French production of the Concorde airliner, Toulouse has a fine cathedral, with a good flea market nearby, and several buildings well worth visiting.

A hired Caribbean passes a loaded barge on the Canal Latéral a la Garonne. (picture: Hugh McKnight)

182

From Toulouse you resume your passage via the Canal Latéral a la Garonne. This follows the course of the river itself fairly closely until Castets-en-Dorthe, where the canal enters the river, which has by now changed its name to Gironde. It runs from here to Bordeaux, a convenient place in which to stop in order to step masts. The river runs down to meet the sea at Port Bloc and Royan.

The Canal Latéral a la Garonne has more depth of water, more head-room under the bridges, and runs without the serpentine undulations of the Canal du Midi. There are fifty-three locks, dating back to 1856, the year the canal was opened to navigation, having taken eighteen years to construct. The design of the locks is such that a current tends to push you into the locks and another tends to push you sideways just as you emerge from the exit gate.

Locks on this canal are being automated. A four-signal light is seen when you approach one of these locks. There are two red lights on the left and two more on the right, and a red and white pole hangs from a wire across the canal. Two red lights indicates that you must wait. When they change to one red and one green approach the pole and turn it. When you get two green you can go ahead. You will find a red light on the lock gate ahead which changes to green when the gate opens itself. There may be a delay while the level is changed inside the lock so that the gate can be opened.

When you are inside the lock someone has to go ashore to tend the warps in the usual way. He also has to close the gates, which he does by pulling the red knob on the small handle on the cabin on the lock side. When they are closed the forward gate will start to operate itself. When the four pistons on the gate are fully up another tug on the red knob will open the gates, and you have three minutes in which to get out before the gates close.

If you find that you have a choice of two poles to operate outside the lock the rule is that the left hand pole is for descending craft and the one on the right is for ascending craft.

If two vessels are approaching, a red and green might change back to two reds, indicating that the craft coming the other way has priority. If this happens resist the temptation to nip into the lock before the gates close, because the whole three minute sequence, including the closing of the gates and the changing of the lights to two reds must be completed before a twist of the pole starts it all happening all over again.

The first few miles out of Toulouse sees a busy road and a railway closely following the line of the canal. These two alternative transport systems make it very difficult to find

An aqueduct on the Canal Latéral a la Garonne.
(picture: Hugh McKnight)

184

Lady lock-keeper on the Canal Latèral a la Garonne – the hat not just for decoration. (picture: Hugh McKnight)

somewhere peaceful to stop for the night. However, if you leave Toulouse reasonably early in the day you will have plenty of time in which to select a good parking place.

Just before Moissac the canal crosses the river Tarn, running through a quarter mile long viaduct. It isn't every day you can be in a boat on one waterway and look down and see another a long way below you!

Moissac itself is a very attractive little town with a cathedral and some interesting cloisters. A good safe mooring is available alongside one of the quays in the town.

Another day's run takes you to Agen, which is where the prunes come from, and almost immediately afterwards you cross another aqueduct, this time nearly six hundred yards long. On this section of the canal you come to some of the automated locks, a series of four.

Finally you enter the Bassin des Gares, which is the place you have been looking for! From here, you pass through the final lock, and into the river.

Here again there is a problem of depth of water over the sill when you leave. The river being tidal there can be considerable difference in the level on the river-side of the lock, proven by the design of the lock-keepers house which has an outside staircase which goes up and up and up to make sure that the lock-keeper has access to the top story of his house when the river is in flood.

It is best to take the advice of the lock-keeper or a barge skipper. You will probably find that the convoy sets out with you at the tail end at just about high water.

The current in the Gironde is fierce. Many people will advise you to take a pilot as far as Bordeaux in view of the unpredictable meanderings of the channel. There is really little need to take one, providing you obey the traffic signals under the bridge and follow meticulously in the wake of the deep-laden barges. Make sure you pick ones which are going all the way to Bordeaux.

Most yachts should be able to carry a tide as far as Bordeaux, where there is a substantial net-work of docks. It is probably best for you to tie up outside the big lock which the large commercial ships use to enter the docks until you can lock in with them on the new tide. The lock is on the port side a little after an impressive stone bridge and before

The lock in to the dock complex at Bordeaux.
(picture: Hugh McKnight)

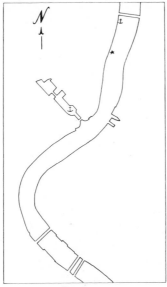

Bordeaux.

the very high bridge which spans the river a little further downstream and under which the big ships can pass.

A characteristic of the Gironde is the occasional appearance of a small tidal bore, *le mascaret,* presumably caused because the incoming tide is held up by the current of the river in the opposite direction.

When you are tied up by the lock entrance the arrival of this bore can create a brief period of surge and swirl which requires doubled warps to make sure you don't get swept away unexpectedly.

The lock-master at Bordeaux will direct you to a berth just within the commercial dock complex where the traffic will not disturb you and where you will be able to step your masts in comfort. If a crane is required he will assist in arranging it.

The bridge just below the docks area is a suspension one which may cause slight alarm when you look at it because an optical illusion can make you think you will never clear it with your masts. Don't worry, just compare the height of your masts with the height of the masts of the commercial shipping in the docks!

7. The Bay of Biscay

Not as bad as its reputation would have you believe
Before leaving Bordeaux overhaul the engine, gear, the safety
equipment, everything. Check the ground tackle, the warps,
fill up with water, fill up with fuel. The invaluable Shell
credit scheme operates in Bordeaux, and delivery will almost
certainly be by bowser.

Make sure that your copies of Adlard Cole's three books
on cruising in Biscay and North Brittany are to hand. Without
them the problems of navigation and pilotage in the next
stage of your dream trip will be increased a hundredfold. The
books are entitled *North Brittany Harbours and Anchorages*
and *Biscay Harbours and Anchorages, volumes I and II.*

You must pay great attention to the weather forecasts
from now on, especially if your passage coincides with the
Equinox. You should be able to pick up the BBC without
any difficulty, which is of enormous assistance, and you
should always err on the side of caution in deciding on what
you are going to do next.

The tides also call for great attention, a new discipline
after the lack of tides in the Med.

It is a good plan to make notes before the start of any
passage; listing the times of tides at various places en route;
the times at which the harbours you will pass will be acces-

sible to you in case of emergency; the estimated time of arrival at various landmarks on the way and the likely state of the tide when you reach them; radio beacons and their call signals; all the information you may need in a hurry.

All this is because the first part of the trip takes you across the upper half of the Bay of Biscay, which is not always as bad as its reputation would make you believe, but which can be a very bad place indeed in which to be caught out if it starts to blow.

General map of Brittany

The most likely place to make as a jumping off harbour for the tricky passage through the Raz de Sein and the Chenal du Four is Audierne. Take the trip to Audierne a step at a time, remembering that there are plenty of harbours in which to shelter if it should blow up, and most of them are reasonably close together.

With all the experience you will now have behind you, even if you were a little unsure of yourself at the start of the trip back in the UK, by now you will have had more practical yachting than many people achieve in a life-time of week-end boating.

You may begin to understand the slightly amused tolerance with which many professional seamen like fishermen and tug skippers treat yachtsmen. They do it all the time for a living, and have forgotten more than many yachtsmen will ever learn.

The run down the Gironde deposits you at the mouth of the estuary with a choice of harbours in which to stop, Royan on the northern side of the estuary and Port Bloc on the other. Royan is favoured by many people because it caters for yachtsmen, is larger, has good facilities and is further to the north, whereas Port Bloc is a small commercial port with virtually nothing in the way of facilities. It has no great charm, but the local people are friendly, and it is usually possible to find a berth alongside a dredger or fishing boat.

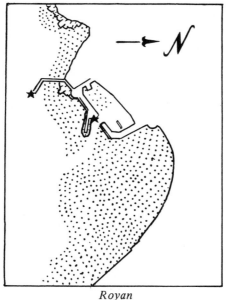

Royan

The actual run down the Gironde provides a good introduction to the problems of working the tides, if you have become rusty. You must carry the ebb, which can reach 3½ knots, and not put yourself in the position of having to fight the flood any more than you need. The distance to Royan is a little greater than to Port Bloc, which may be an additional reason for favouring the latter. The river itself is well buoyed, and is a doddle as far as finding your way is concerned.

The estuary of the Gironde can be a highly dangerous place when the weather is unfavourable, natural when you think of those fast and complicated tidal streams, the long fetch of the seas across the Atlantic, the effect on them of the shoaling waters and the swell which is often created by a distant and probably now defunct disturbance. It is a good place to get clear of as soon as possible.

To discuss the pilotage of the next leg of your journey in detail would produce several long books, but the following notes should be of value, especially when read in conjunction with Adlard Cole's books.

Where you head for next will be dictated to a certain extent by such factors as wind direction, tide times and streams, your own speed through the water and the extent to which your desire to make long passages survives a few days of actually making them.

It is better to make for harbours which are situated on the eastern side of the off-lying islands rather than on the more exposed western shores of the mainland.

La Rochelle is one well-protected harbour on the mainland, a fascinating place to visit, but only accessible when the lock is open, from one-and-a-half hours before high water until one-and-a-half hours after.

An alternative is St. Martin-de-Ré, a very interesting old town on the Ile de Ré, where there may be just enough water at low water neaps to enable you to lie in the entrance to the inner harbour, you will then be able to make a departure when you choose, and without having to lock out. If the weather should become bad and an unpleasant swell start entering the harbour, which happens when it blows outside, you can always lock in when the gates open.

Another likely harbour is Les Sables-d'Olonne, twenty-eight miles further on, with St Gilles another fifteen miles further on still and Port-Joinville nine miles after that. Port-Joinville is on the Ile-d'Yeu, and is the burial place of Petain. The lock at les Sables-d'Olonne is open for three to four hours at high water: St Gilles dries out: so does Port-Joinville. The degree to which they dry out depends on whether tides are neaps or springs, so it is worth making a few calculations to see if you can expect to have enough water to float you, even though at low water springs the whole harbour may be dry.

Faster or larger boats may try to get from St. Martin-de-Ré

St. Martin on the Ile de Ré.

the seventy-eight miles to Ile de Noirmoutier in one hop, although here again there is the problem of the whole harbour drying out. There is a harbour at Pornic, five miles past Ile de Noirmoutier, a poor one and drying out though it was dredged in 1972, or St.-Nazaire, the famous naval base, about sixty miles from St. Martin-de-Ré.

The harbour at St. Nazaire lies some distance up a long estuary, which means that if you sail up it to the harbour you

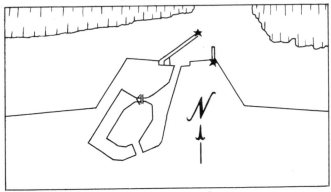

St. Martin-de-Ré

have to sail down it again, which could waste time when your objective really is to get on.

Le Palais, on Belle Ile, a little further on than St.-Nazaire, is another possible harbour, with an inner harbour which has to be reached by locking-in. The outer harbour dries out, inevitably.

But there are many harbours along this coast, and the facilities available are improving all the time. Benodet, on the Odet river is a very popular yachting centre, with very good facilities and excellent shelter for a small boat.

Alternatives to Benodet are Port St. Nicholas, on the western end of the Ile de Groix, too exposed to be recommended in anything but good weather; Loc-Maria on the south side of the island, exposed and drying; and Port-Tudy on the northern side, a good safe harbour except in a northerly or north easterly breeze.

Other harbours in the area include:- Lorient, which lies some distance up a river, is well sheltered and offers several mooring places, all described in detail in *Biscay Harbours and Anchorages, Part I.* Here problems arise as a result of very fast tidal streams, and the necessity to work the tides both up and down the river may well reduce the length of the passage you make on the way to the estuary, and again on leaving.

Port du Pouldu, not recommended for about seven very good reasons. Brigneau, Merrien and Douelan, on the Aven river, none of which are recommended either, except on neap tides, when you should be able to stay afloat inside the harbours themselves, if there is room, or in good weather with offshore winds, when it is OK to anchor off. Belon, again not recommended because of drying bars and the resulting problems of timing arrival and departure to fit in with the tides. It is best to arrive on the last hour of the flood. Port Manech, and the Aven river, not recommended for the same reasons as Belon.

Concarneau, certainly a viable alternative to Benodet. It can be entered at any state of the tide, though the approaches can be rough with a strong onshore wind against the ebb. A mooring can nearly always be found with plenty of water for the majority of yachts. Again, *Biscay Harbours and Anchorages, Part I,* will put you right.

Baie de la Forêt, a reasonable anchorage in most weather conditions. Glénan. These are the islands where the world famous sailing school is located. It is a great area in which to go cruising, but better forgotten as far as you are concerned. The islands are off your direct route home, and by now you won't have enough time left to enable you to indulge in excursions. Not even with *Biscay Harbours and Anchorages* will you find it easy to find a safe anchorage here.

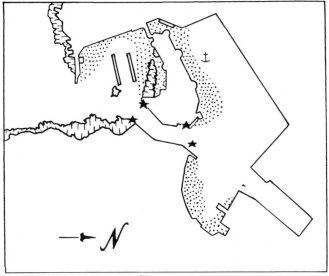

Concarneau

It really is a toss-up, in this neck of the woods, between Concarneau and Benodet, with any number of possible anchorages between Benodet and Audierne, most of which should be avoided unless you can be sure that there will be no onshore winds and no westerly swell.

Most of Audierne dries out, but there is a good anchorage, reasonably well protected, about half a mile to the west and further out, behind the breakwater at St. Evette. It was here that I once picked up a large vacant buoy on the advice of a fisherman. Later the owner of the buoy entered the harbour in a fine large fishing vessel, anchored, and then came over in his dinghy to reassure me that he would be very happy for me to remain on his buoy while he sat on his anchor.

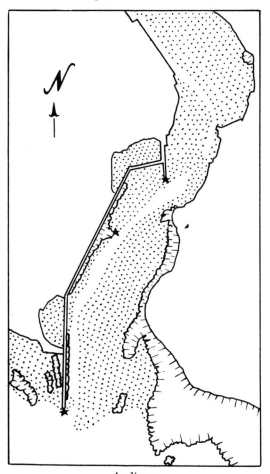

Audierne

This action is typical of Breton fisherman, who must rank very high on any list of the true gentlemen of the world. For some reason they seem to have a fellow feeling for the British, and they will put themselves to an extraordinary amount of trouble to assist a visiting British yachtsman. For this reason they deserve to be treated with a reciprocal degree of courtesy. Their advice is always well worth seeking and always worth acting upon.

From Audierne/St. Evette the next step is to get through the Raz de Sein, through the Chenal du Four and into a nice safe sheltered berth somewhere round the corner.

In good weather — and this passage should only be attempted in good weather — one tide will take you from St. Evette to Aber-Wrach-Paluden with the option of putting into Laberildut or L'Aber-Benoit on the way if you run out of tide or the weather starts to change.

The difficulties in the Raz de Sein and the Chenal du Four are caused by the very fierce tides which occur in the locality, the narrow channels with irregular sea-beds, and what happens when these violent tides are in opposition to strong winds. There are isolated rocks all over the place and at first glance the problems of piloting oneself through this marine jungle are pretty formidable.

With the right weather and a little planning, the passage should be swift and straightforward, however.

First study chapters Three and Eleven in *Biscay Harbours and Anchorages, Part I,* so that you know what you are up against, and then re-read them again closely, keeping the thought at the back of your mind all the time that you will be making the passage in the reverse direction to the text in the book.

These notes may help:-

Audierne	to La Veille lighthouse is 10 miles		(Entrance to Raz de Sein)
La Veille	Pte. St. Mathieu	18	(Entrance to Chenal du Four)
Pte. St. Mathieu	Le Four lighthouse	13	(end of Chenal du Four)
Le Four lighthouse	L'Aber-Wrach	15	
		56 miles	

If you arrive at the Raz de Sein an hour after slack water, which is about four hours after high water Brest, you will have a favourable tide from Audierne to the Raz; the first weak part of the tidal stream will take you through the Raz with the hope of only a moderate sea even if the wind is against the tide; and then a favourable tide to take you through the Chenal du Four — a tide which has not reached its maximum speed, however. Finally, the last of the tide should take you comfortably as far as L'Aber-Wrach.

The great thing is to avoid making the passage with wind against tide, because this kicks up a very rough sea. Slack water lasts for about half an hour each side of the turn of the tide, which is from four hours to five hours after high water Brest when you are heading north.

The channels are all well-buoyed or marked by light-houses, and one problem is to appreciate that the strength of the tide is setting you over the ground at a greater rate than you normally make, and therefore you should not be surprised at the progress you are making and confuse the navigational marks.

If you should decide to make the passage in two legs because of a deterioration in the weather, you have the options of Douarnenez, Brest, Riviere de Chateaulin (a long way out of your way, though), and Camaret, all with good, safe, bad-weather berths. There are a number of other havens

L'Aber-Wrach. A local fishing boat running home in the evening light.

which are only suitable in good weather or in specific wind conditions.

In addition to making the usual notes regarding tide times and so on, a programme of estimated times of arrival at the principal lighthouses and their characteristics is extremely valuable, the physical appearance of each as well as the details of their flashes. Mark on the chart the actual time of arrival, so that you can check back on where you were at stated times if you do become confused by the multiplicity of navigational marks.

North Brittany Harbours and Anchorages, provides very complete instructions for entering either L'Aber-Benoit or L'Aber-Wrach. The former is a little easier to enter, but if you have time and a favourable tide it is better to bash on for L'Aber-Wrach.

At first glance there is an absolutely bewildering profusion of buoys, beacons, painted rocks, lighthouses, stakes, withies and what-have-you. If you get lost you can always luff up, or put the engine into neutral, while you sort all the marks out. The tides will be running at a reasonable speed by now. Pencil the time of arrival at each mark on the Admiralty chart so that you will have a known point and will be making a known speed, and will thus be able to work back easily if you do get lost.

I labour this point because I did get lost myself once in this locality. It took me over half an hour of frenzied activity to realise that my error was in allowing three pages of the Adlard Coles book to blow over when I had just turned a page, and I was thus attempting to identify the actual marks against a completely different set in the book. The moral is to use an elastic band to hold the pages down, and to use the book as an aid while actually you navigate on the Admiralty chart.

It is essential in these waters to know all the time exactly where you are. Take bearings constantly and pin point your position whenever you can. Check on leeway all the time and check that the compass course you are steering is a good one.

This is particularly important now, because you will be travelling at a time well into the autumn. You can expect a number of days when mist or fog will roll in and landmarks

Up the river at L'Aber-Wrach.

may be suddenly obliterated. This is another reason for continuing to pay great heed to the weather forecasts.

From L'Aber-Wrach or L'Aber-Benoit to the Channel Islands, your next objective, is about ninety miles, and the best port to make for is St. Peter Port, with the new marina at St. Sampson a second choice. At this time of year neither of these harbours will be overcrowded with visitors, unlike the summer, when it has been reported that the number of yachts in St. Peter Port is so great that it is possible to reach the shore by clambering from the middle yacht over the others until you step onto the quay.

And if you think that it is too late in the year for this passage to be fun my wife will tell you that it is possible to sunbathe starkers in this area in late October.

If you want to reduce the length of the passage to the Channel Islands you can strike east along the north Brittany shore until you are somewhere near Ile Brehat, when the distance will be about forty-five miles. There are plenty of harbours in which to spend a night along this coast, of which Morlaix and Treguier are two to be recommended.

The pilotage of both is a little hairy, and the longer passage to Guernsey is really a better bet. If you do decide to head along the north Brittany shore *North Brittany Harbours and Anchorages* is absolutely essential.

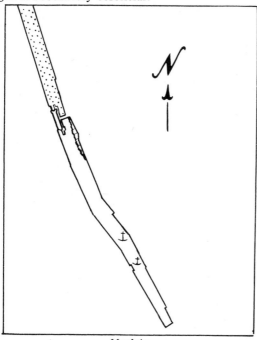

Morlaix

If you want to dodge the hazards of the passage round Brest there is a canal system from near St. Nazaire to St. Malo, which is only open to yachts which do not exceed 85ft 5ins in length, 14ft 9ins beam, have more than 12ft above the water and draw more than about four feet. Again you will have the hassle of lowering and raising masts and for a large number of yachts the limitations on draught are restrictive. Although 4ft is said to be the safe limit there are many people who would say that a more realistic maximum draught is 3ft 9ins. Probably it is best to check at Nantes, on the Loire, where the canal to Redon starts, or at Lorient, where the other entrance into this canal system begins. This meets the other leg at Redon. From Redon it is a straight run

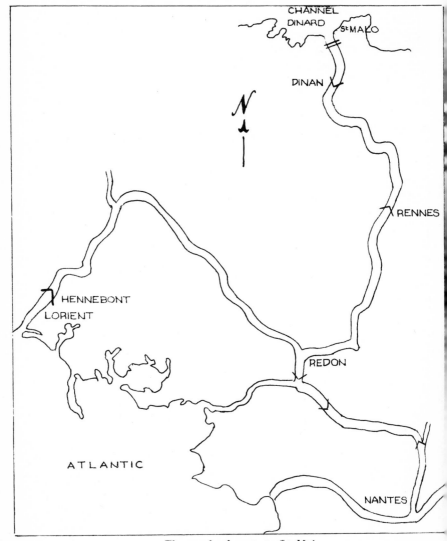

The overland route to St. Malo.

to Malo down the Vilaine river and the Canal d'Ille et Rance. There are an awful lot of locks on this canal system, and I really do not think it is worth the effort.

Back to Guernsey — all the passages you make in the Channel Islands area need to be planned with great attention being paid to the tidal atlas.

From the Channel Islands the best place to make for depends on you and where you are finally heading for. If you are going along the Channel a convenient half way harbour is Cherbourg, with a run of about seventy miles to Yarmouth, Isle of Wight, again a harbour which is dreadfully crowded in the season but which should be reasonably empty at this time of year.

And I guess you won't need me any longer, either.

The author's yacht at the large mooring buoy at Cherbourg.

8. Life Will Never be the Same Again

When you get back to your home mooring and sit and think about it all a whole flood of memories will come pouring in on you. The people you met, the places you visited, the experiences you had, the good times, the bad times, the storms and the calms, the good anchorages and the poor, the heat in the Med. and the fogs of Biscay and Brittany, and gradually you will realise with something of a shudder that the Dream has come to its end.

Now you have to find a job or resume your old one. You have to re-establish your social life, pick up friendships, put down your roots again.

It may prove more difficult than you expect.

Because what is probably the greatest benefit of having attained the Dream is that you have changed fundamentally yourself. You will no longer conform easily in the plastic world in which most of us live. Your standards will have changed, you will question what most people take for granted.

It is unlikely that you will ever again be happy with the 9 to 5 routine and the supermarkets; the values of your friends and acquaintances will no longer be yours. It will be almost impossible to explain any of this to people who have no experience of cruising in a yacht. They will just be on a different wave length: they will have as great a problem in comprehending the new horizons you have acquired as you will have in understanding why it is that they have stayed stuck in their little rut while you have broadened your own horizons immeasurably.

And when you think it all over a few months later you will realise that it was for this reason that you went, and that no matter what problems you find in merging once more into the dull routine of organisation life — it has all been worth it.

USEFUL ADDRESSES

French Railways,
Touring Club de France
French Government Tourist   178, Piccadilly, London, W1
   Office

Royal Yachting Association   Victoria Way, Woking, Surrey.

Touring Club de France   65, Avenue de la Grande Armee,
   75, Paris

Bureau des Transportes   162, rue du Fauborg St. Martin,
Exceptionales   75 Paris 10

Ministere de l'Equipement
   et du Logement,
Direction des Ports Maritimes
et des Voies Navigables,   2e Bureau, 244 Boulevard St.
   Germain, 75 Paris 7

Bureau des Douanes
   pour le Tourism   182, rue St.-Honore, 75, Paris

rough France to the Med.*

Cruising Association   6a, Station Approach, Marylebone Rd., NW1 5LD

Journal de la Navigation   29 Boulevard Henri-IV, 75 Paris IV

Shell International Petroleum Co. Ltd   SPS/3113, Shell Centre, London SE1 7NA

USEFUL CONVERSIONS

1 Litre = 0.22 gallons   1 Gallon = 4.54 litres
1 Kilometre = 0.62 miles   1 Nautical mile = 1.853 kilometres
1 lb. = 0.45 kilos   1 Fathom = 1.83 metres
1 Kilogram = 2.2 lbs

208

FOOD WE TOOK WITH US

(You may think we have peculiar
   tastes)

72 fresh free-range eggs
120 x 1 pt Long Life milk
several packets Ryvita
36 x 1 lb tins butter
12 x 1 lb cheeses
18 x 1 lb jam
6 x 1 lb honey
5 x 16 oz catering packs
   various soups
24 lbs biscuits
48 x 16 oz baked beans
1 x 16 lb catering pack
   cornflakes
12 lbs spaghetti
72 x 1 lb assorted tinned
   fruit
36 tins sardines
6 tins salmon
3 gallons squash

3 large tins cocoa
70 lbs brown sugar
12 bars soap
8 packets washing powder
3 packets Vim
1 gallon disinfectant
48 toilet rolls
12 packets Instant curried
   vegetables
24 tins cream
48 table jellies
6 x 2 lb marmalade
24 small tins tomato puree
12 tins evaporated milk
12 large boxes matches
vast tin of Swarfega
3 lb catering pack raisins
3 lb catering pack sultanas
4 lbs flour

48 tins peas
1 large catering pack dried
  peas
48 x 10 oz tomatoes
36 x 16 oz tinned vegetables
7 lbs rice
6 lbs instant coffee
2 x 1 gallons cooking oil
12 lbs catering quality tea

1 gallon liquid detergent
2 x 6 lbs catering pack prunes
1 cwt. onions
1 cwt. beetroot
1 cwt. red cabbage
15 lbs potatoes
24 packet Soya bean products
  from health food stores

We brought back about a third of this vast amount of food, which helped tide us over the impecunious weeks on our return until we found jobs. There was also a stowage problem, gradually diminishing over the weeks. It is probable that not every reader of this book is as impecunious as we are. There may even be a few people who would like to devote a month or six weeks one year to taking their boat to the Med. and leave it there until the following years when they would spend a month or six weeks cruising around – attaining the Dream on instalments, as it were.

The question arises – where to leave the boat during the winter? Where would she be safe from the vagaries of the weather and the plunderings of local vandals, and where she would be all ready in the following season to take off without any fitting-out hassle?

It is even possible that you might be able to arrange for a modest charter among your friends during the months of the year when the boat is not going to be used by you. It is unlikely that you will be able to arrange many charters any other way.

The sort of place to leave the boat, then, has to be somewhere which is readily accessible by public transport and where there are good facilities and where you can arrange for a reliable person to keep an eye on the boat and do a little maintenance from time to time. This would include topping up the tanks, checking out the engine and victualling ship just before crew joins, as well as running the engine regularly throughout the year, pumping the bilge weekly, touching up the paint and varnish when necessary, and making sure that other boats don't moor dangerously alongside or cause damage and then disappear without leaving a more formal visiting card.

All this adds up to finding a marina where the sort of ship's husband services we have been discussing are readily and reliably available.

One or two places spring to mind. Sète is one, Jose Banus near Marbella is another, Marseilles yet another. Or Porte Borme des Mimosas, which has all the facilities but is not too easily accessible — it is a long ride from the nearest airport.

Alicante is another port where ship's husband services are readily available, even though there is no marina as yet.

The Balearics have a bad reputation as an area to leave a yacht for the winter. This is probably due to the fact that berths are almost invariably stern-to, with the result that a really good long blow can result in a yacht breaking out her anchor, and once one starts to bang about others drag as well as a result of the impact of the boat next door.

In a marina this should not happen, because the boat should be in a berth where she is tied up alongside a pontoon.

The alternative is to find a berth in a fishing harbour and do a deal with a reliable friendly fisherman. Human nature being what it is this is not a course of action which is to be recommended.

People do report having found a safe berth in a canal and having had no troubles after finding a reliable local to undertake the ships husbandry, but I would hesitate to suggest this or suggest places where it would be a good idea to do so.

Gibraltar could be a fine place in which to leave a yacht for a winter, in the marina, and hang the expense. From Gib. you can make four- or six-week cruises every year in several directions, and Gib. is very easy to reach by air.

North Africa is one area where you would be ill-advised to leave a boat unless you have cast-iron local contacts to keep an eye on her. The risk of theft is too great otherwise.

There are the new marinas on the south coast of France, the Languedoc-Roussillon developments. Here, and hang the expense again, you should be able to desert your yacht for several months of the year with no fears. After all, the majority of boats in these marinas appear to be used very little, so the management must be accustomed to looking after boats in their owner's absence.

Remember that if you do leave your boat in France for more than six months it will attract an importation tax unless you take steps to avoid it. Contact Directoir Generale des Douanes, Centre de Reseigniments Douaniers, 182, rue St. Honore, 75, Paris 8eme.

Index

213

214

215